INDUSTRIAL PALIMPSEST:

THE CITY OF NEWARK, NJ

BEST
HEATS
OIL

OIL
COASTAL
COMPANY

COVER IMAGES: (front) Hoffman Beverage Company rooftop bottle, 1930, (back) Newark factory, possibly for a leather product, Charles F. Cummings NJ Information Center, Newark Public Library

FRONTISPIECE: Storage tanks for the Oil Coastal Company, 1983, Charles F. Cummings NJ Information Center, Newark Public Library

Published by
Nina Rappaport/Vertical Urban Factory
www.verticalurbanfactory.org

With work from students at Kean University School of Public Architecture, Union, NJ
www.kean.edu

Distributed by
Actar
440 Park Ave. South
New York, NY 10016
www.actar.com

Authors: Nina Rappaport and Andrew Engelhardt
Copy editor: Jamie Chan
Design: Concept was created by Marta Tonelli and developed by Andrew Engelhardt

ISBN: 978-1-63840-015-8

Printed in the USA

INDUSTRIAL PALIMPSEST: THE CITY OF NEWARK, NJ

NINA RAPPAPORT
ANDREW ENGELHARDT

CONTENTS

Worker in the diamond die department of Wilbur B. Driver Company

PREFACE

This publication is an outgrowth of graduate and undergraduate student work at the School of Public Architecture at Kean University. It is also the first book from the school. In a series of courses students researched sites, analyzed the past and current state, and imagined new futures for former industrial sites and buildings in the city of Newark. In different classes, students focused on Newark and Paterson, N.J. and Newburgh, N.Y. where the students also investigated new hybrid industrial programs. The premise of the first classes was to make industrial history visible as an alternative interpretation to the standard plaque on the wall designating a historic landmark and instead create ideas for outdoor exhibitions, murals, and interactive propositions reflecting on the work of Janet Cardiff, Marc Crinson, Cao Fei, David Gissen, Dolores Hayden, Barbara Kruger, and Damon Rich among others.

Some Newark industrial sites that we studied maintain their productive use, albeit with smaller and lighter industries, and others have been remediated, spurred by zoning changes from industrial to residential, or part of Urban Enterprise Zone programs for real estate incentives. Those that were demolished or decayed remain as brownfields (seven hundred of them in 2010) and still pose a major hazard to future development as they fall into the category of Superfund sites that cost too much for most developers to invest in required remediation. These sites are often underutilized as parking lots, having missed an opportunity from a city agency or financial backing for development.

The civil unrest of the 1960s left Newark with a shrinking population, depleting resources, and infrastructural damage that still remains today. Properties were abandoned and vacated as potential job sites moved to the hinterlands like so many post-industrial cities around the globe. The forgotten industrial architecture heritage, a vessel for the history of entrepreneurship and labor, was too quickly turned into trendy industrial loft spaces, museums, or tourist attractions. While many of these sites are still vacant in Newark, an opportunity exists to make history visible in on-site displays and to revitalize their sites into new sustainable productive spaces. Perhaps a new awareness of what was once there will stimulate a way to integrate sustainable production in renewed urban ecosystems that foster an exchange between place, work, and living in a new symboisis.

In these classes at Kean University, students were asked to research industrial processes, industrial architectural history, and then investigate a specific Newark company. They were challenged to make industrial activity visible through an on-site concept that could potentially be implemented in the future. This publication includes the history of Newark sites that the students analyzed in depth, along with a series of additional historic industrial buildings in images showing the city's huge number of production enterprises. The students' projects respond to the industrial palimpsest—layers of industry shifting and disappearing over time—and produce active and alternative strategies of historic documentation, visible historic interpretation, and adaptive use through analysis and synthesis in their design concepts that include outdoor museums, murals, installations, vending machines, information distribution through objects, recreation of objects, and artifacts on site. The hope is that we can implement some of these projects in the communities in various forms. From the invention of M&M's and pushpins to a center of leather and jewelry production through expansion at each World War, Newark's industrial heritage is revealed.

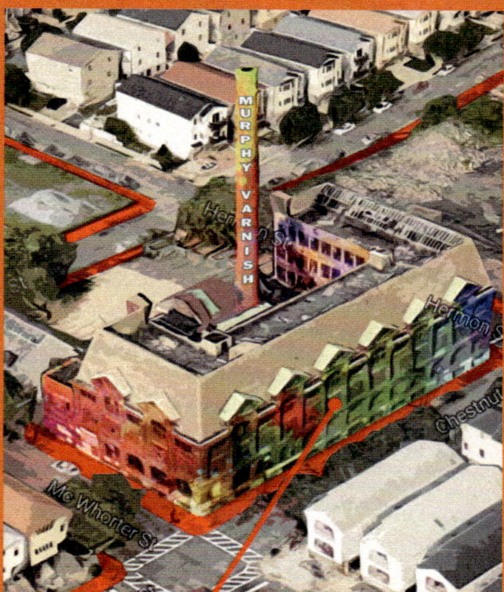

Selected student projects

LEFT TO RIGHT:
Vineyard City, see page 52

The Newark Milk Project, see page 34

Shifman Scaffolding, see page 96

Murphy Varnish Color Scheme, see page 86

Westinghouse Outdoor Exhibit, see page 120

Wiss and Sons Exhibit, see page 132

Acknowledgements

This book was a great collaboration, I would like to thank the students whose work is featured here; James Brett, Gabriel Castillo, Meagan Davis, Daija Ford, Laurent Gutierrez, Bridget Hernandez, Alexander Jimenez, Joseph Ong, Charles Raimondo, Matthew Serrano, Elijah Wagner, and students Sean Boud and Yazmine Graham who did additional research. Great appreciation is given to our Dean David Mohney and Chair Craig Konyk of the School of Public Architecture at Kean University who supported these history/theory classes. Our research would not have been possible without the New Jersey Historical Society and the New Jersey Public Library whose archive was a treasure trove and whose librarians, Beth Zak-Cohen and Tom Ankner, provided support to our students to conduct research. We are thankful to Hanini Group for their contribution to make this work become a publication and their efforts at preserving Newark's historic architecture. Jamie Chan, our copy editor, helped to make the language clear and Marta Tonelli created the design template. We would also like to thank colleagues Tony Schuman, Damon Rich, and Michael Calafati and the work of Newark native Myles Zhang as well as the companies who let us into their factories and provided information. Rather than extensive footnotes, we have included comprehensive research documentation and further reading in the Resources Section in the back of the book.

Industrial Building
Rail
Future Planning

INDUSTRIAL PALIMPSEST: NEWARK

NINA RAPPAPORT

View down Broad Street, 1892

OPPOSITE: Map of Newark factories, 1873

Newark, which was officially granted city status in 1836, followed the pattern of development of so many waterfront industrialized cities, transitioning from farms to factories in the 1700s to 1800s, as did nearby Paterson and New York City. Industry harnessed natural resources such as rivers for mill power, converted steam power to electricity, and built infrastructural networks such as canals and bridges for ships, railways, and roads to distribute goods (which later enabled the development of intensive logistics hubs). With numerous inventors among its residents, Newark established itself as an industrious boomtown.

In the first Industrial Revolution of the late eighteenth and early nineteenth century, Newark—a city of making—required vast and numerous workspaces. Company owners constructed factory after factory in brick, reinforced concrete with steel sash windows, and endless smokestacks that punctuated the city's puritan grid mesh. A series of industrial clusters developed along the Passaic and Hackensack rivers moved inland with the construction of the 1831 Morris Canal that ran from Lake Hopatcong to Newark and Phillipsburg, N.J., linking through inland waterways that reached all the way to the coalfields in Lehigh Valley, P.A. Natural resources—apples for cider; hops and grains for beer; tamarack trees for tanning leather; cotton and wool spun, dyed, and woven into textiles; earth metals mined for celluloid, wire, foundries, and extraction enterprises—transformed new inventions into numerous products and byproducts expanding Newark's economies and employment opportunities.

In Newark, inventors such as Thomas Edison established shops and laboratories, which led to revolutionary discoveries. Edison developed new systems for the American Telegraph Works in Newark but his first factory was built in Menlo Park following his patent for the light bulb. This factory was moved to Harrison in 1882 and continued to operate as the Edison Lamp Works of General Electric until becoming a vacuum tube factory for the Radio Corporation of America in the 1930s. A local rival of Edison's, Edward Weston, created a dynamo for electroplating which sparked the Weston Electric Light Company. The company went on to pioneer new arc lighting systems that illuminated the Brooklyn Bridge when it opened in 1883.

Seth Boyden established the first American factory for patent leather after reverse-engineering and improving the process from European products while Frank Waterman created a disposable pen in his Thomas Street factory, which was later occupied by a company that made glass eyes for dolls and, even later, zippers. Isaac Banister, with his son James, created a large shoe company. Metal making industries were also important to the local economy, including Tiffany & Co. plated silver, Krementz & Company jewelry using precious metals, and Edward Balbach Sr. development of a more efficient process for separating precious metals from the lead alloys that companies like Tiffany and Krementz discarded.

Chemical industries made celluloid, varnish, and paints that polluted Newark's rivers. Beverage companies quenched the public's thirst via twenty-six breweries that thrived in the 1880s; among them Ballantine, Krueger, Wiedenmayer, and Pabst Blue Ribbon. Flour mills and baked goods, candy and chewing gum, and milk and butter companies capitalized on the city's dynamic and expanding population. Companies in Newark contributed to the development of a total supply chain of every good that the local community, New York City, and the wider world desired to consume, earning the city the nickname "Brick City."

Outside of the city's industrial center, affluent neighborhoods sprawled with the proliferation of single-family homes. Weequahic and Forest Hill developed around public parks. In 1895, Branch Brook Park began development as the country's first county park which expanded in the 1920s after receiving donated land from prominent Newark families such as the Ballantines. The location was scouted by Frederick Law Olmsted but the design was executed by his son and stepson, Frederick Law Olmsted Jr. and John Charles Olmsted. The brothers also designed Weequahic Park, which buffers the industrial corridor Frelinghuysen Ave. from a middle-class residential neighborhood.

The industrial neighborhoods of Ironbound and Central Ward expanded as more and more factories sprang up, integrating work life into the communities. Some companies, such as Krueger and Westinghouse, built worker housing nearby, but, for the most part, workers in industrial jobs toiled long hours, were paid little, and did not live well. Following patterns of employment opportunities in the 1920s with the Great Migration north, many African Americans moved to Newark for the new industrial jobs. By this time, the Morris Canal had become obsolete with the expansion of railways and was converted into a light rail and subway beginning in 1929 with some portions filled in for roads. Where barges once transported factory products and raw materials, one of Newark's two dozen light rail lines now brings suburban shoppers and commuters to downtown. The city's streetcars were replaced by buses by the 1950s but the track along the canal still remains today. The Morris Canal is commemorated, however, in the subway's stations with tile murals by Newark native Domenico Mortellito.

A boat is elevated on an inclined plane to cross High Street (MLK Boulevard today). The Morris Canal was built with twenty-three inclined planes to adjust changes in elevation. Various factories are to the right including Almond & White machine manufacturers and Manhattan Dress Suit Case Company.

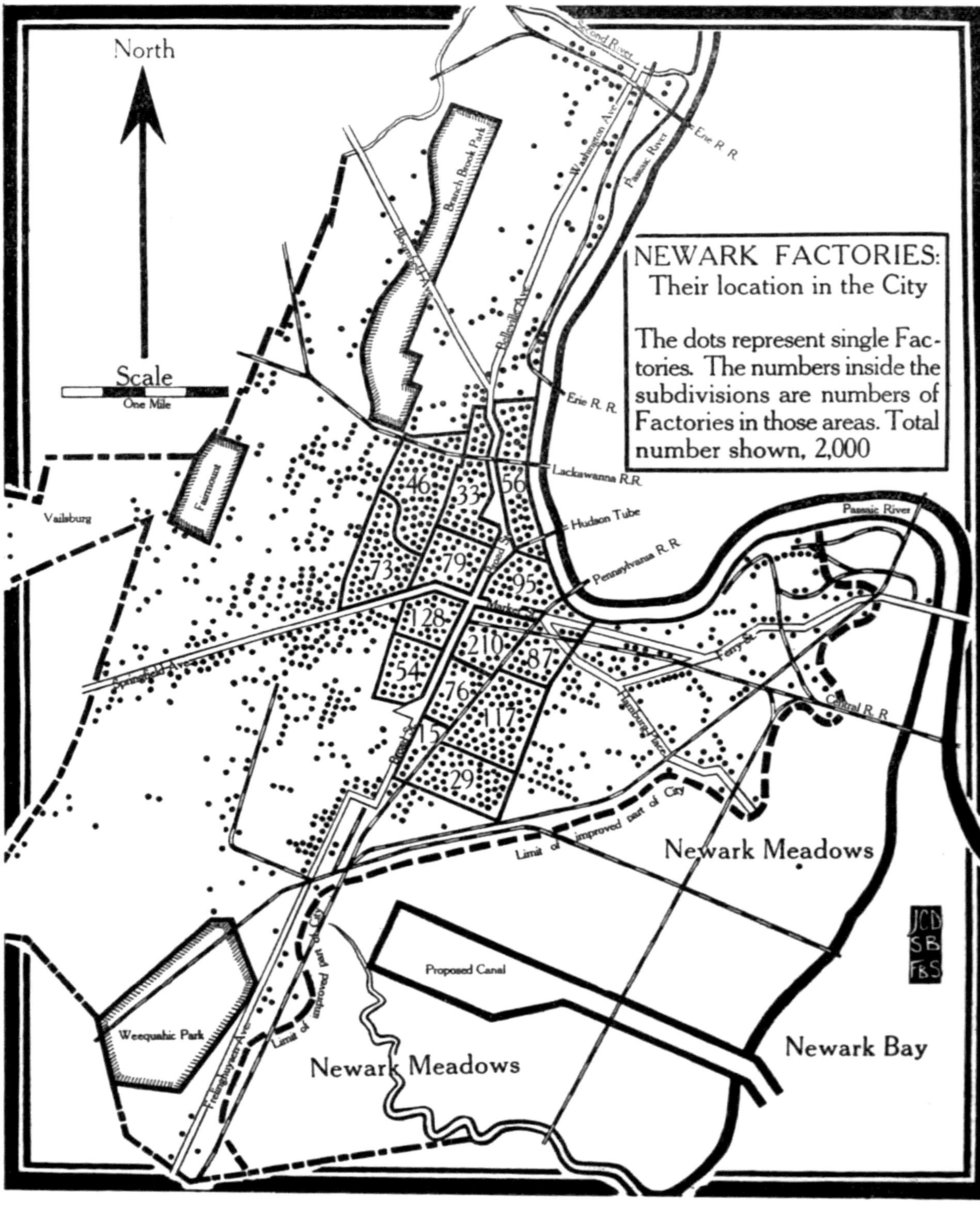
NEWARK FACTORIES:
Their location in the City
The dots represent single Factories. The numbers inside the subdivisions are numbers of Factories in those areas. Total number shown, 2,000
North
Scale
One Mile
Second River
Erie R. R.
Washington Ave.
Passaic River
Branch Brook Park
Belleville Ave.
Lackawanna R.R.
Hudson Tube
Pennsylvania R. R.
Passaic River
Market St.
Ferry St.
Central R. R.
Springfield Ave.
Vailsburg
Fairmount
Broad St.
Hamburg Place
Limit of improved part of City
Newark Meadows
Proposed Canal
Weequahic Park
Frelinghuysen Ave.
Newark Meadows
Newark Bay
46
33
56
73
79
95
128
210
87
54
76
117
15
29
JCD
SB
F&S

From the Civil War to the two World Wars, many local companies shifted from peacetime to wartime production, which increased employment opportunities. New Jersey and its industrial centers sympathized with the Confederacy and Newark earned the reputation as a "southern workshop" for supplying southern troops with leather and other goods. Newark was producing 90 percent of America's patent leather at this time. The city (and state) did not vote for Lincoln. However, post-World War II, following the redlining of neighborhoods and displacement for highway projects, New Jersey—one of the densest states on the East Coast—sowed its production seeds beyond the urban core: Nabisco grew in Fair Lawn, pharmaceutical companies created clusters in New Brunswick and Princeton, and Newark's M&M factory relocated to Hackettstown. Rather than continue as an urban production center, the region around the Newark International Airport, which was adjacent to the Ports of Newark and Elizabeth, became a center for warehousing and logistics.

Due to a series of strikes arising from worker discontent, numerous factories continued to vacate their original homes, further exacerbating the racial and economic divisions that culminated in the Newark Rebellion of 1967; police abuse was the primary catalyst but unemployment, inadequate housing, and decline in social services were also factors. Newark's Division of City Planning's move to build a college in the primarily African American neighborhood of the Central Ward created even stronger social divides that are still being repaired.

While many of these industries are long lost, some of their buildings still exist as the palimpsest of entrepreneurial ventures and capitalistic growth. A spirit of invention continues, albeit hardly nurtured with public economic support. Contemporary businesses can be inspired by the industriousness that was once Newark. In fact, new industry can transform the city into "Nework" today focusing on innovative, sustainable, and cradle-to-cradle production, recycling and reuse efforts, in physical spaces that are smaller. What is happening in Newark is parallel to post-industrial cities throughout the world.

Notable companies have maintained their legacies in Newark, such as Shifman Mattress Company, which continues to make high-end mattresses in the same space they have occupied for over a century. More recently, smaller producers have thrived, including those that we typically see in cities—the F's of food, furniture, fashion, and fabrication start-ups. In addition, there remain many chemical and paint-related

OPPOSITE:
Map of Newark Factories in 1911 (Dana, John Cotton. *The Newarker*. 1.2 December 1911. p. 25.)

industries including Benjamin Moore, printing firms, and larger-scale textile companies. Aero Farms has rehabilitated former industrial sheds to grow salad greens; small brewers are capitalizing on Newark's brewery traditions; Union Made is a thriving garment manufacturer.

Organizations such as the New Jersey Industry Partnerships and the Newark Workforce Investment Board, as well as the city's economic development department and Chamber of Commerce, are working together to support new enterprises, as other organizations did in the past, steering away from low-paying service jobs toward innovating jobs that incorporate advanced technologies and Industry 4.0. This offers industry a way to retool both factories and workforces. Ultimately, at this moment in time, in cities across the country, workforce education and training are key to industry's continued development and viability.

As Newark establishes these new industries, the city must also face remediation of brownfield sites left by former factories. In 2019, the EPA selected Newark for an $800,000 Brownfields Multipurpose Grant to assess sites for hazardous substances and petroleum contamination, develop cleanup and reuse plans, and conduct cleanup activities. The city's focus for this grant is the 1,250-acre North Ward of the Newark riverfront, which is centered around a heavily industrialized area along the Passaic River. Priority sites include the Seton Leather Company, a former leather manufacturing facility; and Q Petroleum Incorporated, a former heating fuel oil transfer station.

A brownfield site that was part of the Murphy Varnish Company (see page 80) where tract housing was also built in the late 1990s. In 2020 a development broke ground that expects to provide seventy-two apartments.

LEFT TO RIGHT:
Paints and Colors costume for the Industrial Dance, part of Newark's 250th anniversary celebration, 1916

Clay, Hides, and Leathers costumes for the Industrial Dance, 1916

Robert Treat (Newark's founder) pageant costume, 1916

Making History Visible

The challenge to contemporary historic preservationists, and thus to our students who represent the next generation of urbanists, is to decide what to preserve and how to keep the memory of these production spaces alive without being nostalgic, reductive, idealized, or focused on the company owners who are in the privileged position to write their own histories. How do we discover what happened in the factories, who worked there, how workers were treated, why companies left the city, how much they polluted, and who cleans it up? Ultimately, we are asking whose history are we displaying? These are all questions that the students kept in mind as they created new ideas for Newark's communities manifested in murals, exhibits, landscapes, and prototype objects.

One urban design and spatial planning idea that can assist in this equitable growth, and is both historically relevant and future-forward looking is the reassessment of hybrid potentials to mix light industry with other uses, which has been part of the Newark City Planning code since 2015. This means that a brewery located next to residences and light industrial uses can be combined with production spaces, an example that parallels the earliest rise of the factory in residential communities in the nineteenth century is transformed into clean, green industries in the present day. The mix in use can also point to a new direction for revitalizing communities by building new programs within production spaces integrated with job training, skill-building, and education. They can exist alongside manufacturing processes for a visible and productive future.

OVERLEAF:
Selected Factories, Newark, NJ
Google Earth

SELECTED FACTORIES, NEWARK, NJ

1. BALBACH SMELTING & REFINING COMPANY
2. P. BALLANTINE & SONS BREWING COMPANY
3. BORDEN DAIRY COMPANY
4. CLARK THREAD COMPANY
5. CRUCIBLE STEEL COMPANY OF AMERICA
6. HANOVIA CHEMICAL & MANUFACTURING COMPANY
7. JAMES A BANISTER COMPANY
8. MURPHY VARNISH COMPANY
9. SHIFMAN MATTRESS COMPANY
10. TIFFANY & CO.
11. WATTS, CAMPBELL COMPANY
12. WESTINGHOUSE ELECTRICAL COMPANY
13. WISS & SONS COMPANY

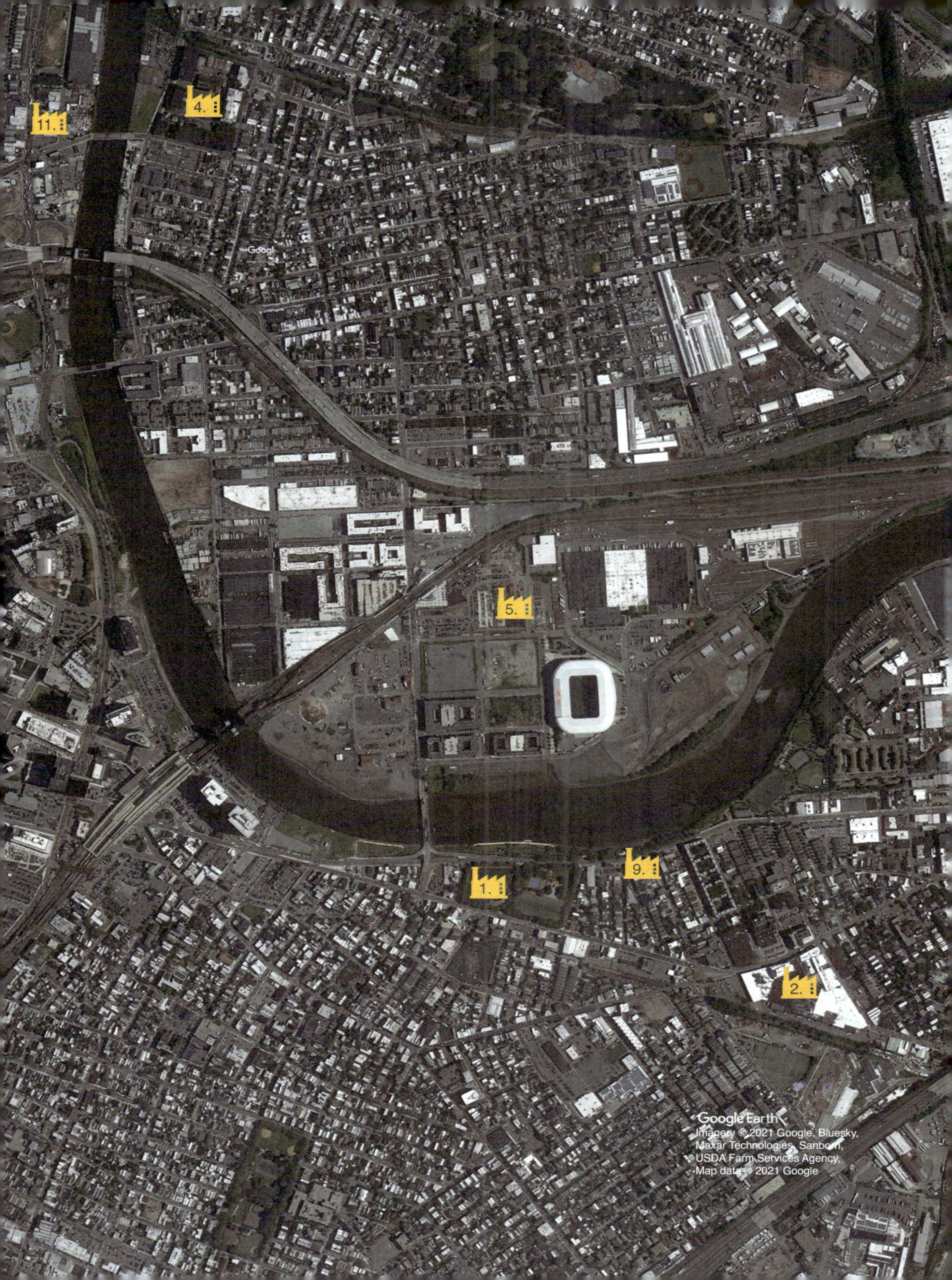

11.
4.
5.
1.
9.
2.
Google Earth
Imagery © 2021 Google, Bluesky, Maxar Technologies, Sanborn, USDA Farm Services Agency, Map data © 2021 Google

BALBACH SMELTING & REFINING COMPANY

Illustration of Balbach Smelting and Refining Company factory complex, 1875

The Balbach Smelting and Refining Company was the first commercial electrolytic refinery in the United States. It was the second largest metal processing enterprise in the country until it closed in the 1920s. Edward Balbach Sr., a German immigrant who made metal bullions from gold and silver dust collected from the numerous Newark jewelry shops, patented a more efficient process for separating gold and silver from lead in 1865.

Lead was softened in a reverberatory furnace, followed by a liquidating furnace, and then desilverized by the addition of zinc in a kettle. The gold-silver-zinc-lead alloy was separated and then distilled in a tilting retort, condensing about fifty percent of the zinc for further use, resulting in a rich, gold-silver-lead bullion, which was then placed in a shallow container called a cupel and heated to refine the metal further.

In 1881, the company began manufacturing copper, which was used for cables following the invention of the telegraph and telephone. Edward Balbach Jr. ran the company until his death in 1910. Edward Randolph, a longtime employee and Balbach's son-in-law, inherited the company and managed it for nine years until he died. The factory closed in the 1920s as ore extraction facilities moved outside of Newark.

The factory complex began with a desilverizing department on a narrow stretch of land between the Passaic River and the Morris Canal, with additional buildings along Passaic Avenue (now Raymond Boulevard).The complex grew to cover almost two blocks between Van Buren and Ferguson Streets with a copper department on the southern block.

Riverfront Park, originally called Newark's Mayfair Park, was adjacent to Balbach and intended to be a relaxing retreat for factory workers advocated for by Franklin Murphy of the Murphy Varnish Company (see page 80). Essex County purchased the lot and extended the park between 1926 and 1931 to include a baseball field on the site.

The park continues to grow with the renovation of Newark's riverfront including a dynamic design stretching along the Passaic River lead by Damon Rich of Hector, formerly in his role as Planning Director and Chief Urban Designer for the city of Newark. Featuring designs by Mott MacDonald, Weintraub Diaz, and graphic designers MTWTF, the new riverfront was part of a redevelopment plan the Newark Municipal Council adopted in 2013. It also culminated in the Newark Riverfront Revival (NRR) which is an organization aimed to reconnect residents with the Passaic River.

Former Balbach Smelting & Refining Company and Wiedenmayer & Son's Brewery, 2020

Google Earth

Imagery © 2021 Google, Bluesky, Maxar Technologies, Sanborn, USDA Farm Services Agency, Map data © 2021 Google

P. BALLANTINE & SONS BREWING COMPANY

Illustration of the Ballantine Brewery complex, 1905

OVERLEAF:
Home of Ballantine Ale and Beer postcard

The P. Ballantine and Sons Brewing Company was founded in 1840 by Peter Ballantine. After emigrating from Scotland to the United States, Ballantine and his partner Erastus Patterson opened the company in Newark under the name of Patterson & Ballantine Brewing Company. They rented their first factory building and almost a decade later, Ballantine bought out his partner and purchased a new site at 137 River Street near the Passaic River to establish a new factory. There, with the aid of his three sons, the company was re-established as P. Ballantine and Sons Brewing Company in 1857.

The company continued to produce various ales, growing into one of the largest beer production companies in the United States by

1879. During this time the company expanded and established a second brewery in Newark to brew a new lager. Simultaneously the company adopted what would become its iconic logo, three interlocked rings, representing Purity, Body, and Flavor.

After the death of their father in 1883, the three sons managed the company in turn. Following generations inherited it for a number of years, beginning with George Griswold Frelinghuysen, the son-in-law of Robert H. Ballantine, which marked the second age of the Ballantine brewing company.

The company was faced with its largest challenge in its second era. The 18th Amendment to the United States Constitution was ratified in 1920, prohibiting alcohol in the United States and forcing the Ballantine brewery to consolidate and reduce the production of various beers, and instead produce other goods such as malt syrup to remain in business. During this challenging time, the company managed to stay in business but when the 21st Amendment repealed the 18th Amendment in 1933, the damage had been done and the Ballantine family sought to sell. The company found itself in the hands of the Badenhausen brothers, who saw the company through its most profitable and successful period—it became a sponsor for the New York Yankees and the number three beer in the United States.

Unfortunately, the period of success gradually saw a decline in profits in the following years. Eventually, the brothers sold the company to the Falstaff Brewing Corporation, who closed the Newark brewery in 1972, leaving 2,300 workers unemployed. They opened doors elsewhere, until they too sold the company, this time to the Pabst Brewing Company, where it is currently functioning as the Pabst company's craft beer, known as Ballantine IPA, having relaunched in 2014.

During its successful and challenging enterprise, the Ballantine brewery grew to cover 40 acres of land with a capacity of five million barrels. The complex included countless structures to encapsulate the entire production process such as brewhouses and mills, wagon sheds, wash houses, ice plants, a shop for carpenters and coopers, immense storage facilities, and a brewmaster's house. There was also a shipping depot on Ferry Street that connected to rail in a series of spurs belonging to other owners feeding into the Newark and New York Branch of the Central Railroad of New Jersey. This patch of land was eventually covered by Ballantine's 725,000 square foot conglomerate building bound by the rail and Ferry and Christie Streets.

Home of Ballan

View of the new Visitor's Room facing the bar where guests are served Ballantine Ale and Beer with light refreshments.

ne Ale and Beer

Truly a small city—covering 34 acres. Modern buildings designed for the specialized tasks of brewing, fermenting, storage and bottling. Railroad sidings where trains unload the raw grains and hops at Ballantine's doorstep—and where great lines of box cars are loaded with the finished product starting America's finest on its journey all over the United States and to many foreign lands.

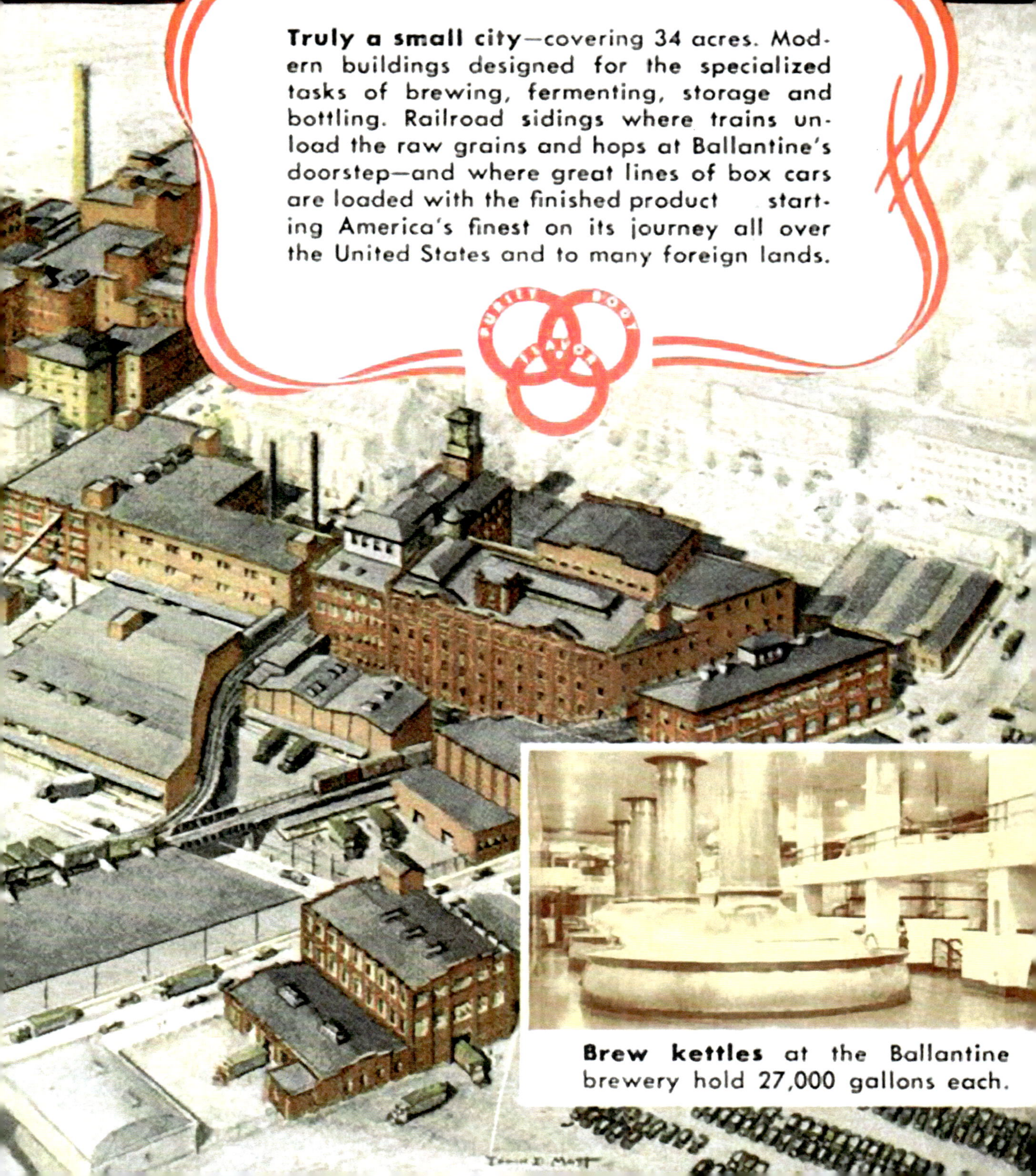

Brew kettles at the Ballantine brewery hold 27,000 gallons each.

Ballantine silos and railroad tracks in 1960 before construction of new buildings

Warehouse truck and freight loading docks, 1937

One of its additions that later aggregated with other buildings is a 1937 bottling plant and warehouse designed by J. Sanford Shanley. It is a reinforced concrete and masonry building with an elaborate spiral conveyor to distribute cases and kegs into storage and then onto loading docks. An office space once housed clerical workers, the manager of the shipping department, and a paymaster.

The exterior of this small structure is similar to many of the brewery buildings of this time, exuding a sense of efficiency and cleanliness with streamlined features such as flat roofs, rounded corners, and horizontal windows in an Art Moderne aesthetic. The red brick running bond includes protruding brick bands that adorn the simple building volumes. The bottling plant has seven massive circular louvers assisting in ventilation along Christie Street. The metal awning and adjacent loading dock tower have a rounded corner; accenting the building's massing but also echoing the form following the function as this rounded corner hugs the spiral conveyor inside.

FACTORY PROCESS

The P. Ballantine and Sons Brewing Company outlined its production process in their own company newspaper, *The Three Rings*. It included a schematic diagram showing the conveyance of dry materials to the bottling and cooling process for bottled beers and the flow of draught beer to be barreled.

Dry raw materials for beer production, such as cereal grain like barley, corn, or rice, hops, pure water, and brewing yeast, were placed in a device known as a mash tub and cooker, where they were distributed in proper proportions to water. The next ingredient, malt, was drawn from its storage where it underwent a cleaning process, several weighings, and was crushed before being added into the mash tub with the raw ingredients. At the same time, a specific amount of corn grits were weighed and sent to the cooker, along with a small amount of malt to liquify the grits. As all of these ingredients were mixed in the mash tub and pumped into a lauter tub.

Once pumped into the lauter tub, the liquid passed through a filter bed and was drawn from the bottom of the tub. Remaining amounts of water were extracted from the leftover grains by washing them with hot water run through sparging equipment. The liquid, a combination of fermentable and unfermentable sugars, is called wort. Wort was then collected in a brew kettle and is boiled with hops for flavor, clarity, and to aid in its preservation during the fermentation process.

After this boiling was completed, the hops were filtered out through a strainer and the remaining grains were carried away for cattle feed. This wort was then settled in a device known as a coolship, and

Storage and the sprial conveyor in the warehouse, 1937

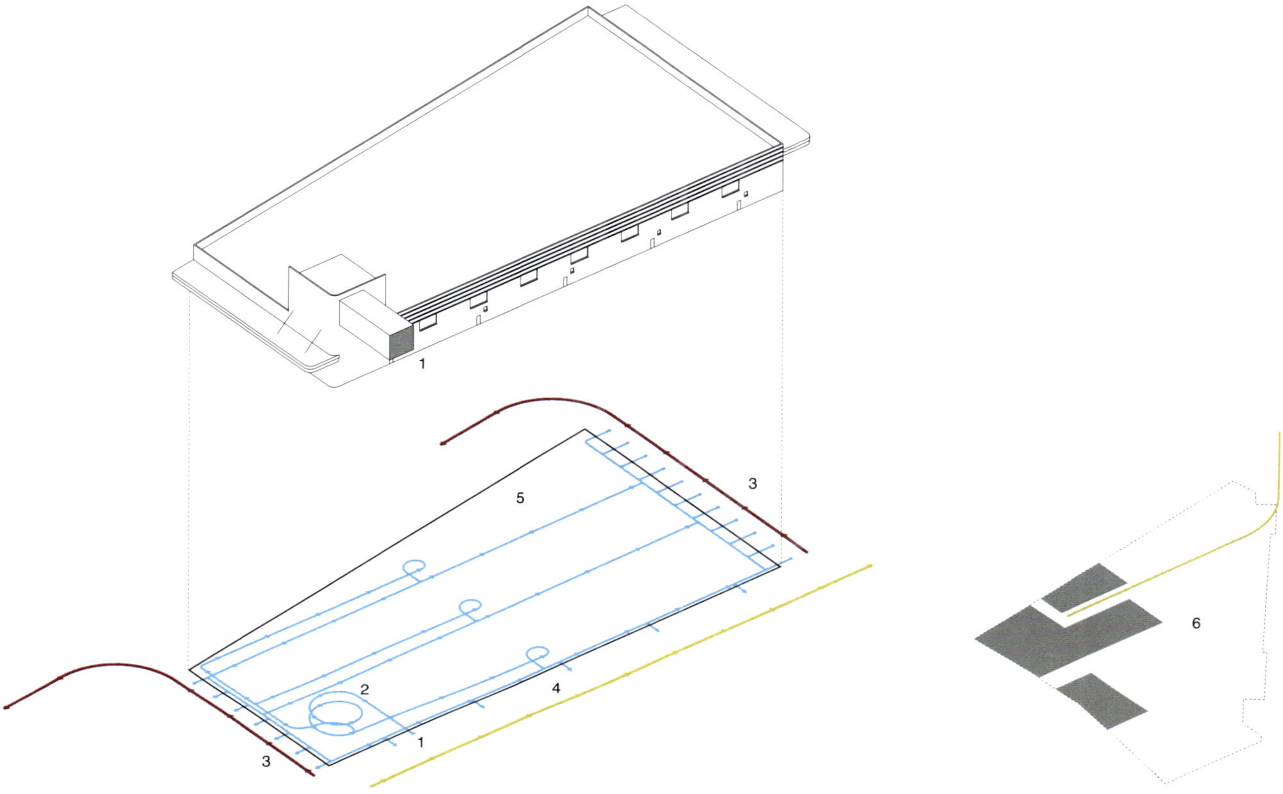

Isometric loading and storing process drawing

KEY:

1 Cases and kegs are transported from the filling plant over a conveyor bridge.

2 A spiral conveyor with switch distributes them.

3 They are loaded onto trucks.

4 They are loaded onto freight cars.

5 They are also stored here.

6 Some of the facilities in the 1930s with the outline of the building in 2020

- The Beer Cases / Kegs
- The Trucks
- The Freight Cars

passed over a series of cooling devices before flowing into starting tanks, where the brewer's yeast was added to the mixture. Fermenters, open and closed, allowed for carbon dioxide gas to be collected and compressed, and utilized to adjust pressure and gas volume in the bottling plant.

Following the fermentation process, the brew was cooled again before being passed to a storage tank. The beer was tested and aged, before going through more cooling and filtration. The product was then sent to the finishing tanks, filtered once more, and sent off to one of two locations. If the beer was being sent to the bottling plant, it was further cooled. If it was instead going to be sold as draught beer, it was passed on to a racking cellar and put into barrels.

Cases and kegs of beer reached the warehouse on a steel bridge that extended over a freight rail. The spiral conveyor distributed the beer to the appropriate storage area until being loaded for shipment. Extensive conveyor belts penetrated the exterior wall and extended below a metal awning serving loading docks on three facades of the building. The docks accommodated freight cars, large trailer trucks for long distance shipping, and smaller, lighter trucks for local deliveries.

CURRENT CONDITION

Former Ballantine Brewery building, 2020

OPPOSITE:
Former Ballantine Brewery building, 2020

Former sprawling buildings of the Ballantine brewery are alive again with industry. Now referred to as the Ballantine Industrial Complex, it has one million square feet of industrial and loft space including the 725,000-square-foot building at 397-447 Ferry Street. This massive building shows signs of its expansions over decades, including concrete silos that puncture the common roof line and the 1937 bottling plant and warehouse which received a second floor addition and buildings that abut the former three loading docks.

Turnbridge Equities purchased the property in 2019. The investors subsequently spent over $10 million dollars in repairs and modernization efforts including roof and window replacements, yard and loading area repaving and extensive aesthetic upgrades. The largest building contrasts the other red brick buildings of the complex with a striking coat of blue paint. The original iconic Ballantine logo is still visible, fixed above the main entrance on Ferry Street.

54
NO PARKING

Ballantine silos before renovation

Former Ballantine Brewery building, 2020

The complex is a multi-tenant industrial space that was quickly occupied, indicating the need for industrial space and the infrastructural benefits of Newark. Current tenants include a commercial moving company, a restaurant supply store, a clothing retailer warehouse, a paint applicator factory, and an umbrella factory.

Some structures were demolished for housing in the early 2000s. A 2021 proposal for a 280-unit mixed-use development would replace a former brewery building at Freeman and Ferry Streets. The existing building is consistent with the complex with its accentuated bands of brick that align to the grids of the warehouse windows. A patch in the southeast wall reveals where a steel bridge once extended over Ferry Street. A clock formerly there was relocated to a nearby wall.

The relocated clock, 2020

NEWARK'S BREWING & BOTTLING INDUSTRY

ANHEUSER-BUSCH/BUDWEISER

BAIER & HILL'S LAGER BIER BREWERY
333-345 SPRINGFIELD AVE

BIRKENHAUER & BAUMANN'S BREWERY
194-202 S ORANGE ST

DUBOIS BREWING COMPANY
308-312 JELLIFF AVE

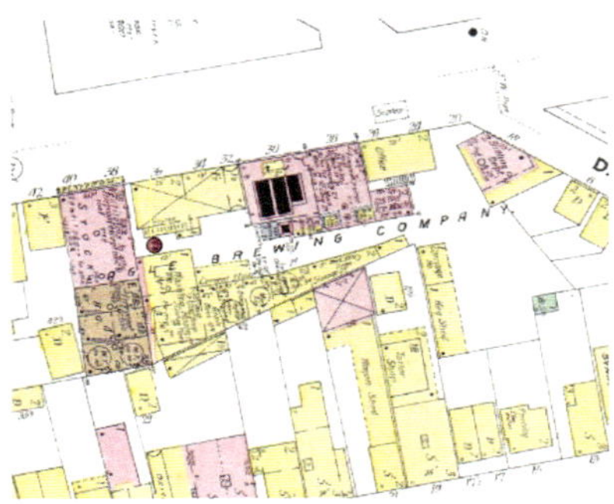

EAGLE BREWERY
20-40 HAYES ST

ESSEX COUNTY BREWING COMPANY
63-85 CLIFTON AVE

HOFFMAN BEVERAGE COMPANY
384 S ORANGE AVE

HOME BREWING COMPANY
320-332 ORANGE ST

KRUEGER'S BREWING COMPANY
75-101 BELMONT AVE

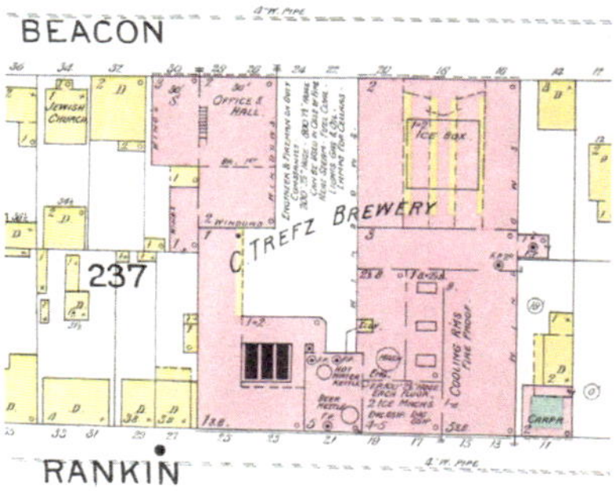

C. TREFZ BREWERY
16-30 BEACON ST

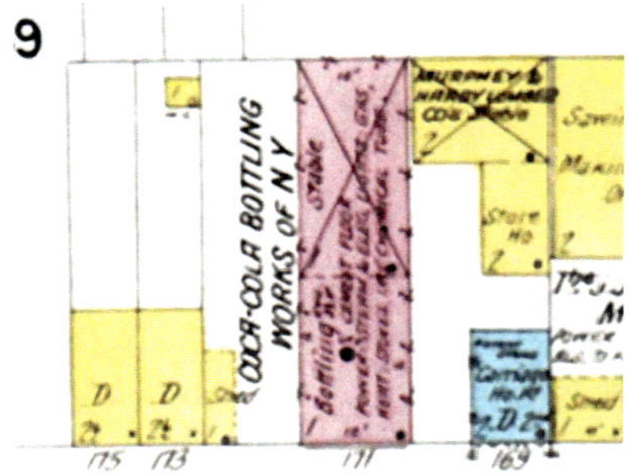

COCA COLA BOTTLING WORKS
171 OGDEN AVE

DEMETRIO LOPRETE, BOTTLE-MAKER
189-203 FRELINGHUYSEN AVE

FIEGENSPAN'S BREWERY
317 ORANGE ST

PETER HAUCK'S BREWERY

JOSEPH HENSLER BREWING COMPANY
73 HAMBURG PL

MORTON & BROTHER BREWERY
235-241 HIGH ST

PABST'S BREWERY
384 S ORANGE AVE

WEIDENMAYER'S & SONS BREWERY
124-126 HAMBURG PL
588 MARKET ST

BORDEN DAIRY COMPANY

Borden Dairy Company milk plant, 1955

The Borden Dairy Company is a major dairy company that has transitioned with new products and branding over its hundred-plus years. The company continues to take pride in the founder, Gail Borden, and the brand's mascot since 1936, Elsie the Cow.

Originally called the New York Condensed Milk Company, the company achieved success with the production of sweetened condensed milk, which could be stored and transported without refrigeration for longer periods of time. This was an advantage during the Civil War when the Union Army was supplied with condensed milk. An image of an eagle was used when it supplied soldiers with wartime rations during the World Wars. The company produced a short film in 1942 describing milk production processing during World War II, referring to it as white ammunition: the "powerful defender in the constant battle for better health." Following Gail Borden's death in 1874, the company added processed milk and evaporated milk to its brand and renamed the company, the Borden Company, in honor of the founder.

In Newark, Borden built a milk plant in 1928 on the corner of Orange and Nesbitt Streets. Here, workers pasteurized milk from nearby farms and distributed milk bottles to Essex, Union, Morris, Hudson,

Building elevation detail

Bergen, Passaic, and Somerset counties. Designed by the firm of William E. and David J. Lehman, the building is a Neo-Byzantine style design of beige brick with stone details. The intent was to avoid the appearance of a factory and instead construct a simple yet dignified building. The architecture firm had also built the Alderney Dairy factory and some notable Newark buildings including the U.S. Trust Building, the U.S. Post Office, and the Federal Court House. In 1978, the Lehman Architectural Partnership designed the Temple B'nai Abraham synagogue in Livingston, N.J.

The three-story concrete frame building had 114,500 square feet of floor space. A covered wagon yard that accommodated two hundred delivery wagons occupies 30,000 square feet of the second floor at the Orange Street side. One hundred and thirty horses that pulled the wagons lived in stables and had an adjacent feed room, hay loft, harness room, veterinary surgeon's office, and ramps that connect this upper floor to the covered yard.

The design of the building is eclectic with motifs similar to Byzantine mosques on the eastern side with a rooftop structure that housed a water tank. It is anchored by four finials that resemble minarets and windows on the second level are framed with Solomonic pilasters. An ornate frieze above the window opening with pediments features carvings of mythical creatures and eagles protecting a milk bottle in the center. The decorative elements and tower served as identifying landmarks for the facility presenting an austere stature with some lighthearted touches.

Borden Jr., Gale. "Vacuum Pan." Patent 2,103. 14 November 1865.

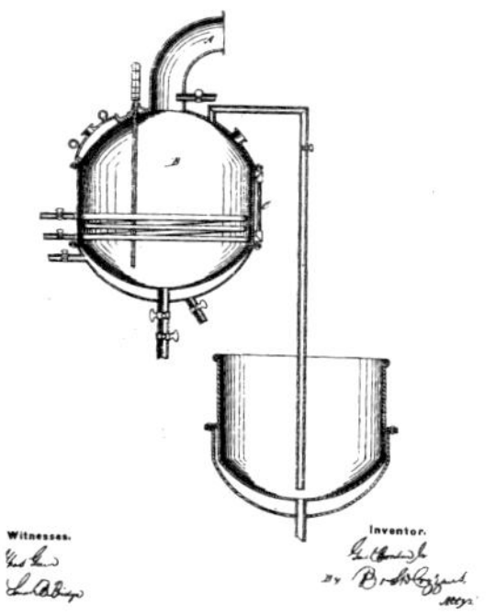

FACTORY PROCESS

Gail Borden invented the process for creating this sweetened condensed milk in 1856, and was responsible for numerous inventions and patents. The historic company literature referred to him as a man "born a hundred years ahead of his time." He even played a role in the planning of Houston and Galveston, T.X.

Raw milk was transported from local farms via train directly to the rear of the factory. The Borden Company invented insulated, enamel-lined tank cars for milk transport. The milk was then weighed to monitor how much product was entering the plant and then stored. Special pipes used filtered, compressed air for circulation so that the milk was never exposed to air from the tank car to the individual bottle.

The pasteurization process began with heating the milk to approximately 145°F for thirty minutes and then cooling it to 40°F. The milk then flowed through filters and onto the bottling and capping machine. The pasteurization equipment had a capacity of moving 9,600 quarts an hour and the facility produces 80,000 quarts of milk on a typical day.

The milk then flowed to the bottling and capping machine, which used glass bottles sterilized in the four automatic washing machines. This machine could automatically seal sixty bottles per minute. The milk bottles moved along a track like "an army of glass soldiers equipped with their quota of white ammunition" until they were placed in crates for delivery.

The crates traveled along a 650-foot-long conveyor to transfer them to the covered yard and go out for delivery. The covered yard above the pasteurization floor included cold storage in the center where drivers loaded their horse-drawn wagons to deliver milk. The million-dollar facility attracted visitors who could see the process from a mezzanine viewing gallery.

In *The Pioneer Maniates of Newark*, a book following Greek immigrants at the beginning of the twentieth century, Kiriakouli Yiorgouleas, or Charles Gergulas as he later identified as, recalled his experiences as a delivery man for the Borden Milk Plant in the 1920s. He described the horse as knowing the route—when to stop and when to turn.

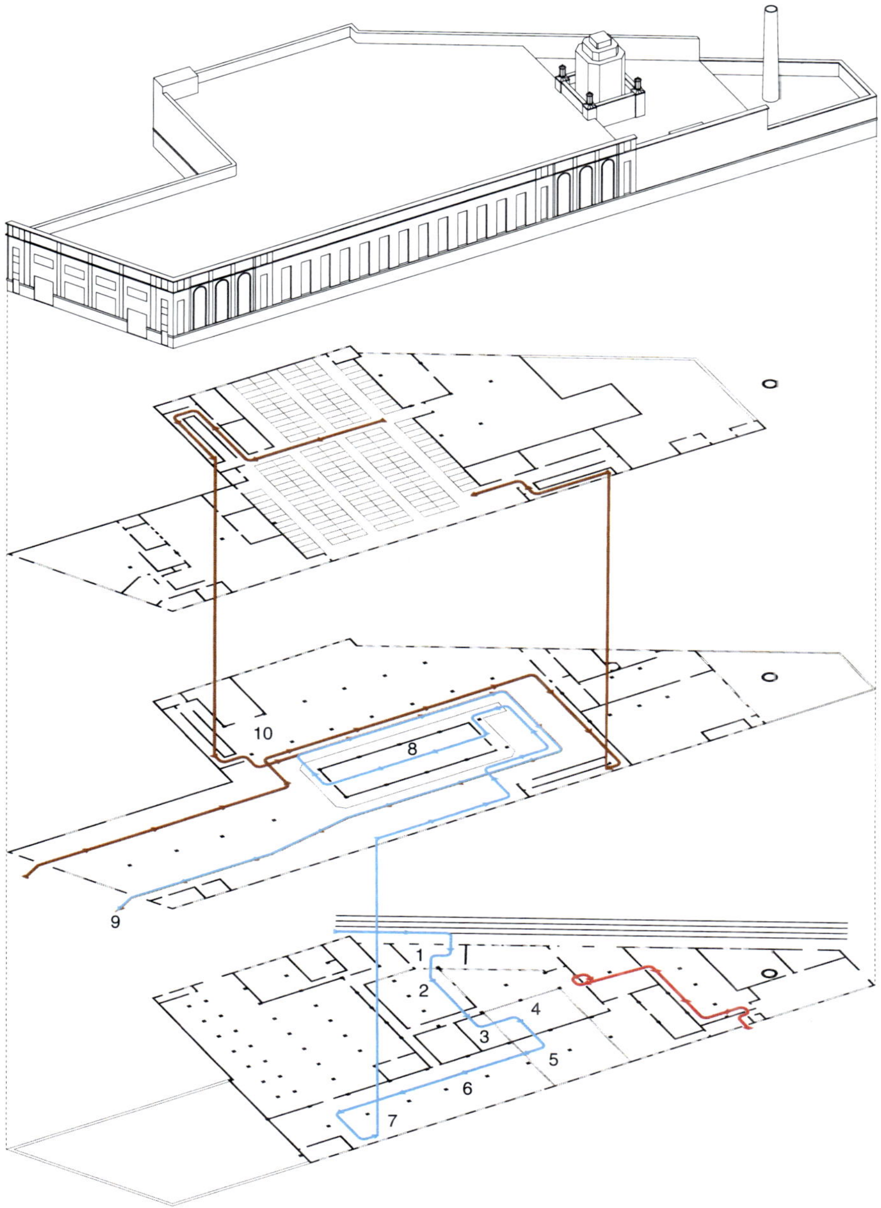

Exploded isometric factory process drawing

KEY:

1 Raw milk is weighed

2 Raw milk is stored

3 Raw milk is heated and filtered

4 Raw milk is pasteurized and quality tested

5 Automatic machines wash the glass bottles

6 Milk is bottled and capped

7 Milk bottles are loaded into crates and brought up to the covered yard by a conveyor belt

8 Milk crates are stored in a chilled room until loaded onto a wagon

9 The milkman delivers the milk and retrieves empty bottles

10 The empty bottles are collected and taken to the washing machines

The Milk
The Horses
The Viewers

Bottles traveling from the washing machine to the bottle-filling machines on a track

CURRENT CONDITION

Former doorways of the Borden milk plant, 2019

The Borden milk plant closed around 1966. At this time, the company was making major changes; the name was changed to Borden Inc,, the headquarters moved from New York to Columbus, OH, and the chemical division became Borden Chemical with successful products including Elmer's Glue and Krazy Glue. The building became a factory for the New Community Corporation which made prefabricated housing and school components for local developers and school boards. The factory relocated around 2004. Today the building is in disrepair on one side but used by the Newark Department of Public Safety on the other. Concrete block-sealed windows, graffiti-covered gates and walls, and urban nature have claimed the building's openings including the water tank enclosure.

Currently, the Newark Fire Department Training Academy uses this building for emergency and homeland security training and storage. It is also possible that the stables were used for the mounted police's horses before a larger facility was built in the adjacent lot.

Over the years, the site has been considered for many development proposals. In May 2020, Brandywine Acquisition and Development, LLC purchased the property to erect affordable housing on the corner of Nesbitt and Orange Streets and extend along the empty site across the street left by the Baxter Terrace housing project. It is estimated that 1,000 residential units will be completed. Brandywine will also redevelop the Bergen Street Police and Fire Training Academy.

Former Borden milk plant, 2019

BUS STOP
NO PARKING
WHEN ROAD IS SNOW COVERED
OFFICE
BORDEN'S
FARM PRODUCTS
COMPANY INC
98

THE NEWARK MILK PROJECT

ANDREW ENGELHARDT

Stills from *The Newark Milk Project* film *White Ammunition*, 2019

OPPOSITE: Rendering of *The Newark Milk Project* murals

Residents of Newark experienced racial discrimination and police brutality, which erupted in the riots if the Newark Rebellion of 1967, but concerns over the Newark Police Department have prompted a civil rights investigation as recently as 2011. After a three-year investigation the Department of Justice found that black residents were 2.5 times more likely to be stopped and one out of every five uses of force was "excessive and unconstitutional." The police department has since been working towards improvements under federal oversight. *The Newark Milk Project* by Andrew Engelhardt examines the operations of the Borden Company and makes it visible again, applying them to Newark emergency services in an attempt to address established concerns and grievances with law enforcement. Frank Bellina, deputy coordinator of field operations and tactical training for the Office of Emergency Management and Homeland Security has said, "Newark is definitely taking homeland security very seriously. We want to lead in homeland security."

The Newark Milk Project is a temporary installation that aims to unite the community and its local law enforcement. The former factory facade will be painted by local artists as a way to reopen its doors and windows to the lively process it once housed. Milk delivery wagons, factory workers in lab coats, and horses in their stables will liven up this dilapidated building and make the production history visible.

A short film will also be projected onto the building featuring excerpts from the Borden Company's 1942 film *White Ammunition* interlaced with footage of police training videos. The film intends to open a conversation regarding police training and reveals a more sinister meaning to the term "white ammunition."

The John William Smith commemorative milk bottle

COMMEMORATIVE MILK BOTTLES

ANDREW ENGELHARDT

Prototype milk bottle series

The Newark Milk Project will also distribute a limited series of commemorative reusable bottles. The Borden Company began using the glass milk bottle in 1885. It is an artifact of the Borden milk plant that may be found onsite today among the empty spray paint cans and broken beer bottles. The distribution of milk once placed this facility at the center of a network of horse-drawn carriages that extended across five different counties. The Borden milk bottle was essential in providing better health for the community. This service will be memorialized by the production of reusable liquid containers shaped like vintage milk bottles.

The prototype series has four unique labels, each with a QR code that directs users to *the Newark Milk Project* website. The first bottle has no information, only an image of the inconspicuous “mock doomsday” building. The second provides information on the Newark Riots with an image of a *Time Magazine* cover showing a young boy shot by police during the riots. The third bottle is a call to action, asking for suggestions, opinions, and art submissions. The last bottle commemorates John William Smith with his photograph where Elsie the Cow is normally pictured. The Newark Riots erupted after John William Smith was wrongfully and violently arrested. Rumors spread that he was killed by the police officers that pulled him over and a mob quickly gathered outside of the police station.

NEWARK'S DAIRY INDUSTRY

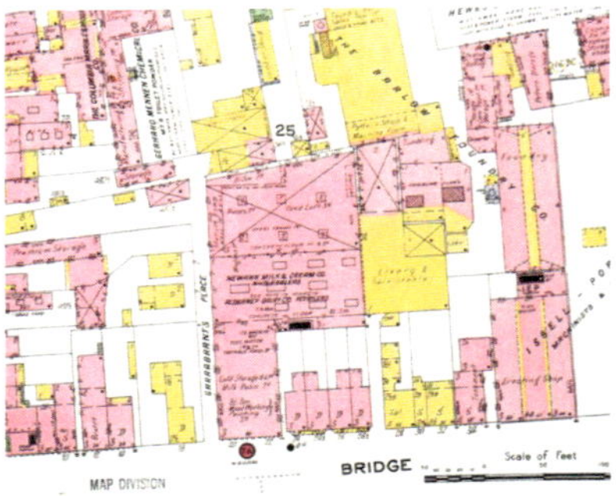

ALDERNEY DAIRY COMPANY
FOUNDED 1894
26 BRIDGE ST

BREYER'S ICE CREAM
444 RAYMOND BLVD

CASTLE'S ICE CREAM COMPANY
68 FABYAN PL

CLINTON MILK COMPANY
351 MORRIS AVE

GREENBORO DAIRY COMPANY
4 ROME ST

NASTO'S ICE CREAM COMPANY
FOUNDED 1939
236-240 JEFFERSON ST

N.J. ICE CREAM COMPANY
303-313, 318-320 MT. PLEASANT AVE

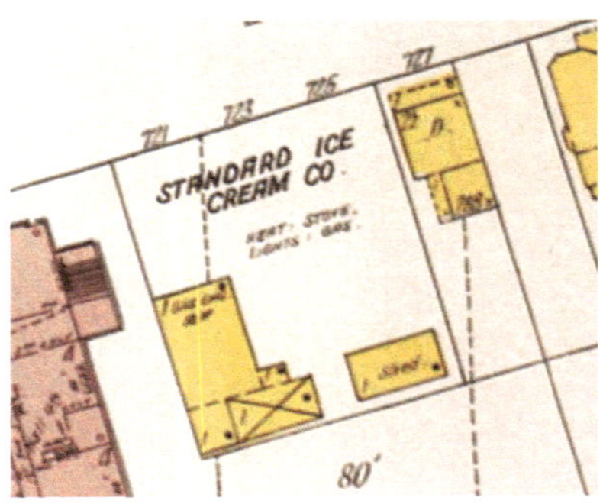

STANDARD ICE CREAM COMPANY
721-725 SUMMER AVE

NEWARK'S CANDY INDUSTRY

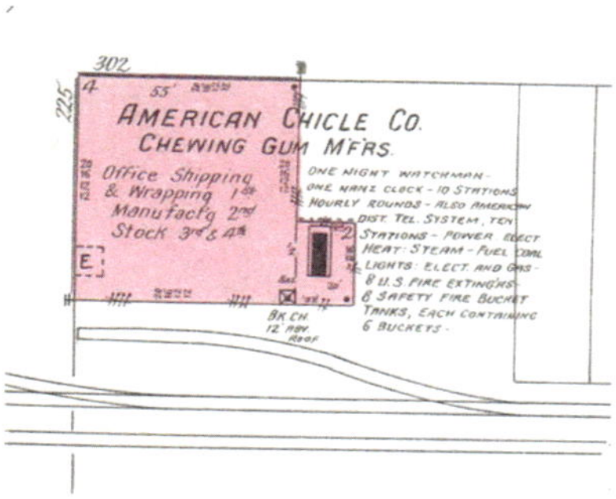

AMERICAN CHICLE COMPANY

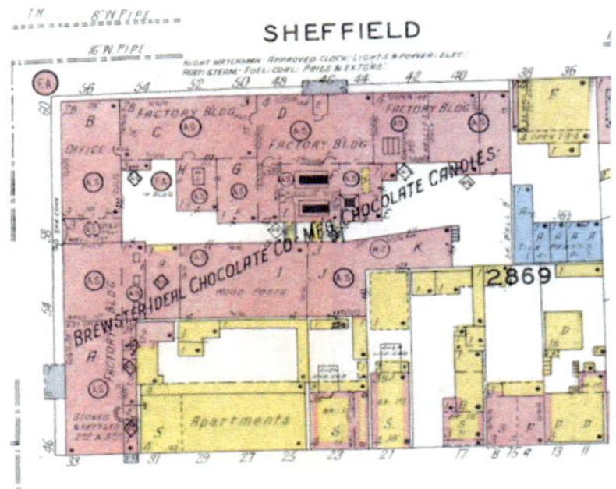

BREWSTER IDEAL CHOCOLATE COMPANY

HOOTON CHOCOLATE COMPANY
341-345 N 4TH ST

THE MANSFIELD COMPANY
227 HIGH ST

MARS WRIGLEY M&M
FOUNDED 1940
285 BADGER AVE
200 N 12TH ST

WADSWORTH CHOCOLATE COMPANY
BUILT 1916
276-290 JELLIFF AVE

CLARK THREAD COMPANY

Southwest view of the Clark Thread Mill, 1977 (Photograph by George R. Adams, AASLH)

The Clark Thread Mill is a notable company in Newark's thread and textile industry and expanded to become the largest thread mill in the United States, and then one of the three largest thread mills globally. After successfully manufacturing cotton thread in 1806, James and Patrick Clark founded the Clark Thread Company in the Scottish town of Paisley. Following increasing sales in the United States, brothers George and William Clark were sent to the United States in 1855 to expand the business. In 1868, a 50,000-square-foot plant was constructed in Newark at 260 Ogden Street. With the waterfront property fully occupied, the company began expanding to the other side of the Passaic River to allow the construction of a bleach house. This expansion continued to provide additional storage and cotton and thread mills.

Among these buildings is a four-story mill erected in 1875. It is located on the southwest corner of the block, which would later be known as the Clark Thread Company Historic District. It is six bays wide and eighteen bays long, measuring about 75 by 400 feet with a gable roof. A majority of the factory's thirty-five buildings were built during the 1880s, accommodating the immense growth the company experienced into the next century.

In the 1900s, Clark Thread merged with several other thread and textile companies, eventually becoming the Coats Group PLC in 1952, the world's largest manufacturer of sewing thread. Clark Thread's contribution to the economic development of Newark cannot be understated; the company grew to be such a force in the thread and textile industry in the United States and the world.

The mill was a complex of four-story brick buildings that housed large thread spinning machinery operated by 5,000 employees. The complex also featured training schools for new employees supervised by senior staff. Other machinery known as pickers, or scutchers, broke up the compressed bales of cotton and removed the bits of unwanted material.

The buildings are still situated on the perimeter of the block along Passaic, Central, and Grant Avenues while the north end fronted the Erie Railroad line. Completed in the 1870s, this train line linked Newark with Jersey City and Paterson. Parts of it are still used for industry in Newark but most service ended by the 1970s. The NX Draw Bridge over the Passaic River has been in the raised position since it was abandoned in 1977.

The interior of the block included additional smaller buildings along with the powerhouse and its landmark smoke stack. The design of this mill complex is organized in a very logical way with the overall manufacturing process continuously traveling via steel bridges. The red brick buildings have Italianate details, including arched windows, various decorative window hoods, a bracketed cornice, and open attics. Numerous belvedere towers stand above the common roofline.

Northwest view of the Clark Thread Mill, 1977 (Photograph by George R. Adams, AASLH)

FACTORY PROCESS

Illustration of the factory before expanding over the Passaic River

OPPOSITE:
Illustration of Clark Thread production from *Scientific American*, 1879

The process for manufacturing cotton sewing thread begins, of course, with the collection process. After raw cotton is collected it is run through a cotton gin, separating the fibers of cotton from the seeds. This ginned cotton is then compressed into large bales and transported to the factory.

The production process began at the Clark Thread Mill in a three-story, 48-by-48-foot building called the picker house. Here, the bales of cotton were run through a machine known as a bale breaker which unraveled the compact cotton using spikes and rollers. It reduced the bales to tufts which could easily be moved onto a conveyor belt by the handful. It was then run through a picker which separated the fibers more thoroughly and cleaned out any dirt that collected during transportation. Afterwards, the material went through two separate scutching processes, which removed remaining impurities from the cotton as it was being prepared for spinning. Finally, a combing machine removed short fibers to improve the strength and quality. The resulting material is known as sliver.

FRENCH COMBERS.
CARDING ROOM.
TWISTING MACHINES.
REELING
SCI. AM. N.Y.

Interior of the Clark Thread Mill, 1977 (Photograph by George R. Adams, AASLH)

The sliver was then put through a drawing process, which straightened the fibers and made them suitable for spinning via a series of rollers. A process called slubbing twisted the cotton fibers. The result of this was a product known as roving, which was a bundle of singlarly long yet uneven fibers prepared for spinning. Following this initial production of roving, it could be put through another roving process to result in a finer product; otherwise it was ready to move on to the spinning process. The production process continued from the picker house to the spinning mill portion of the main factory building along a steel bridge. Sanborn maps reveal an additional cotton warehouse built before 1892 that also connected to the picker house via a steel bridge.

Run through either a spinning mule or a ring spinning machine, the roving would be worked into a higher quality fiber, and would move on to additional steps to become cloth, yarn bundles, or sewing thread. The first process unique to sewing thread was the doubling process, which involved two or more ends of yarn, twisted together to make stronger chords. Clark Thread's products became known as some of the best to use with domestic sewing machines, thanks to the production of their product known as O.N.T. (Our New Thread) which was a six-cord thread strong enough to work with the machines, but not too thick.

The final processes of making sewing thread involved bleaching the thread, winding it, and exposing it to a process known as mercerization, which was a finishing treatment that improved many factors of the thread, such as its strength, luster, and dyeability. The improved sewing thread would be spooled and ready to be distributed and sold to consumers. This manufacturing process was standardized for textiles and fabrics, but largely evolved over time by innovations and inventions that hastened the process, removing the need for hours of hand-picked cotton work and mechanical production.

OPPOSITE:
Interior of the Clark Thread Mill, c. 1900s

Eckhardt, G. R., "Process of Producing a Textured Sewing Thread and a Textured Sewing Thread Made Thereby." Patent 3,153,895. 27 October 1960.

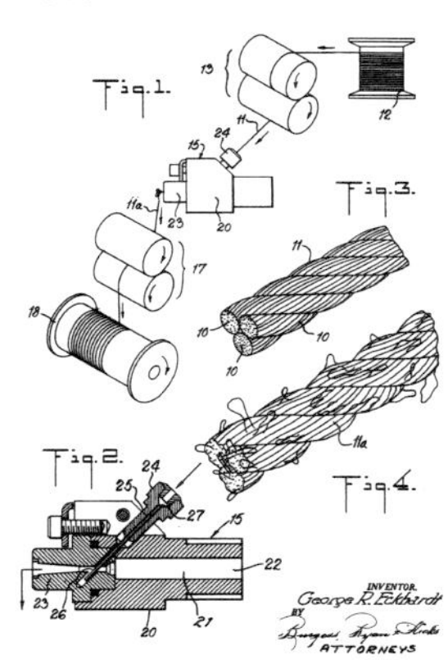

CURRENT CONDITION

Former Clark Thread Mill, 2021

OPPOSITE:
Former Clark Thread Mill building, 2020

The Clark Thread Mill was sold in 1935 but most of the buildings still exist. Owned by the First Republic Corporation of America and known as the East Newark Industrial Center, the buildings were leased to small manufacturers, a majority of which were garment makers. The complex was designated a National Register Historic District in 1978, adopting the name the Clark Thread Company Historic District. This, however, did not protect the buildings from future renovations most notably the replacement with smaller windows and the infilling of openings with concrete blocks.

The Clark Thread Mill is currently in the planning phase for a residential and commercial building by East Newark Town Center LLC, an affiliate of Alma Realty. The 13-acre property will include over six hundred residential units, 91,000 square feet of retail space, and 4,388 square feet of commercial space. Amenities will include a parking garage, rooftop terrace, and tennis courts. Eight of the original structures will be rehabilitated with one- and two-bedroom rental apartments and the smoke stack will be restored.

URBAN STRUCTURES
JOSEPH ONG & GABRIEL CASTILLO

Sketch of proposed *Urban Structure* in University Heights, Newark

The Clark Thread Mill contains approximately four million bricks. It was an impressive achievement in construction that earned a reputation as "one of America's greatest factories" and helped bring recognition to Newark's growth as a large industrial center. The factory also served as a testament to Newark's construction workmanship. Over a thousand workers laid the bricks and the Newark-based Hewes and Phillips Iron Works built the engines that operated the mill.

The Clark Thread Mill was powered by twenty-one steam boilers, each with three hundred horsepower, that relied on a central chimney. Construction began in 1887 but halted for the winter leaving the structure at only eighteen feet in height. Scaffolding surrounding the exterior and a steam powered elevator was erected in the center with a 36-by-42-inch platform providing efficient yet precarious working conditions. It was the world's tallest chimney standing at 335 feet when completed in 1888. A temporary platform was built for visitors to experience the panoramic

Sketch of proposed recreated arch threshold

view of the city before being put to work. It was a feat of engineering assembled from 9,651,899 pounds of brick, 1,000,000 of concrete and 40,000 of ironwork. The pride of Newark, the Brick City, is within these industrial building materials that the student project *Urban Structures* seeks to reclaim.

Urban Structures, by students Joseph Ong and Gabriel Castillo, are public fixtures created from the reclaimed materials of demolished industrial buildings. Initial concept sketches include outdoor garbage cans and reconstructed arches salvaging the brick from the factory for public amenities throughout the city. Various configurations allow familiar elements of industry to occupy Newark once again including arched windows, brick cornices, and smokestacks.

VILLAGE THREADS
BRIDGET HERNANDEZ

A few of *Village Threads*' "hybrid factory" components

OPPOSITE:
Collage for *Village Threads*

Completed in the Hybrid Factory/Hybrid City course, this student project aims to reintroduce urban manufacturing into the city by way of mixed-use design and policy change.

Taking a different, more holistic approach, *Village Threads* by student Bridget Hernandez proposes to reanimate the Clark Thread Mill with a diverse variety of industrial architecture programs. This proposal illustrates the benefits of policy change and current efforts by organizations including the New Jersey Industry Partnerships and the Newark Workforce Investment Board which would allow residential, commercial, light industrial, and recreational programs to coalesce forming a "hybrid factory".

It is an active revitalization effort that differs from surrounding sites in nearby Harrison where industrial architecture is demolished and simply acknowledged with the names of new residential lofts such as Steel Works Apartments or Cobalt Lofts.

Apartments, restaurants, retail, storage facilities, light manufacturers such as jewelers and garment works, and other businesses including car dealerships, tailors, and pet stores will all be unified by the factory's existing perimeter buildings using the central courtyard for recreation and communal use.

VINEYARD CITY
LAURENT GUTIERREZ

Collage for *Vineyard City*

After completing extensive research on vineyards and wine production in New Jersey, student Laurent Gutierrez decided to imagine *Vineyard City*, a vineyard with on-site wine production that also provides housing for the workers. Because it is zoned with a mix of commercial, light industrial, and R-1 Residential with R-1 along the Grant Avenue strip, closer to the existing residential area, there is an opportunity for an interesting combination that supports wine production.

While north Jersey has no vineyards, establishing this business venture in the city of Newark would provide benefits by incorporating production space into residential communities while also bringing green space into a dense, urban setting.

A community farm would provide work for residents of proposed nearby housing for low income families. They can live and work within a historic site and learn the cooperative model with training courses. *Vineyard City* will include offices, a wine tasting café, and community activities to market its products. This student project was also created with the "hybrid factory" in mind.

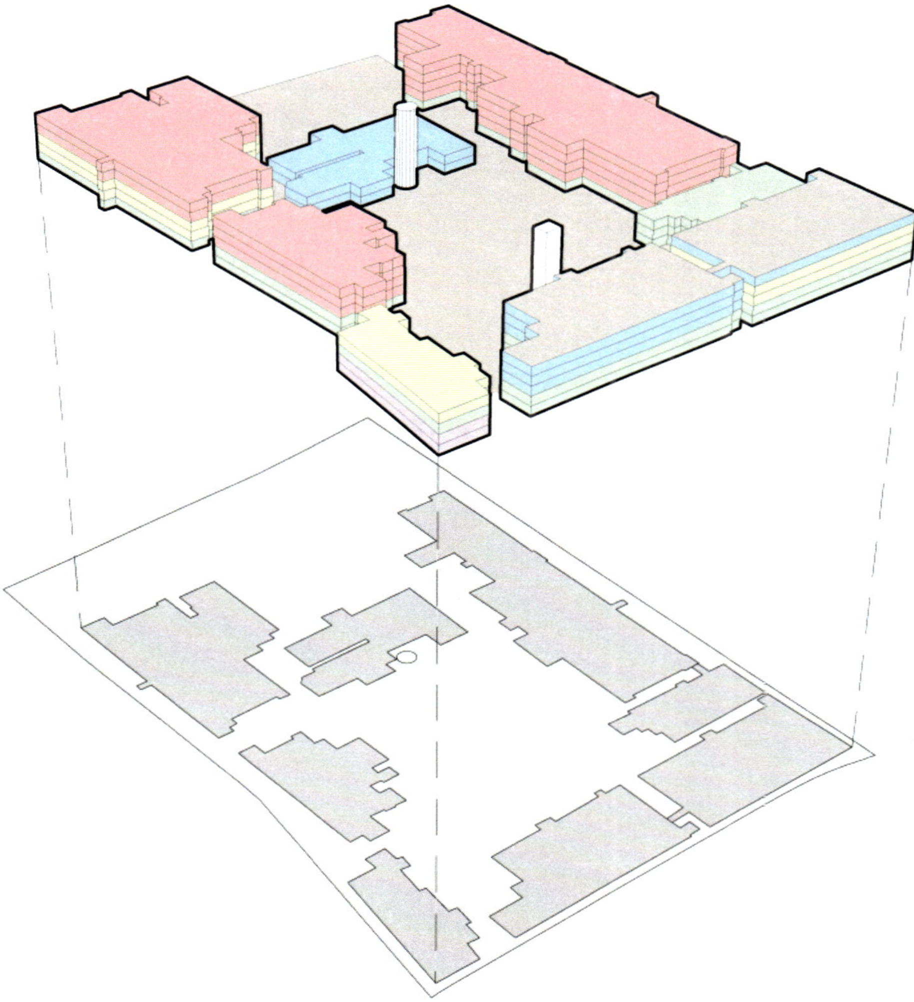

Proposed program isometric drawing

KEY:

Wine tasting

Commercial

Housing

Office

Vineyard

Winery

NEWARK'S THREAD & TEXTILE INDUSTRY

AMERICAN UNDERGARMENT COMPANY
FOUNDED 1883
32-38 GREEN ST

ATHA & HUGHES
FOUNDED 1850

AUG GOERTZ & COMPANY
FOUNDED 1881
278-284 MORRIS AVE

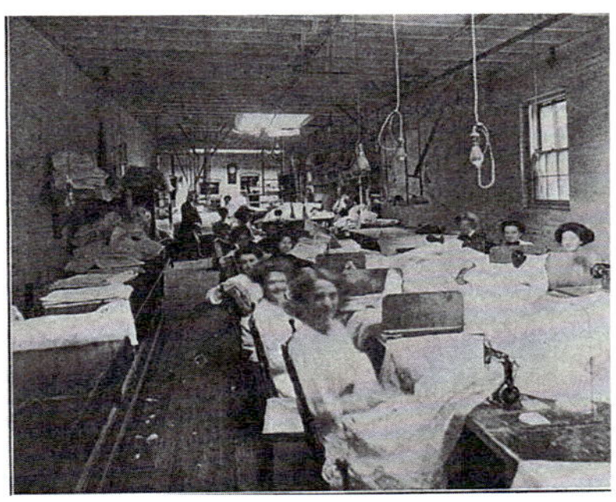

ESSEX LACE CURTAIN WORKS
230 WASHINGTON ST

GIORGIO BROTHERS CLOTHING MANUFACTURERS
223 MORRIS AVE

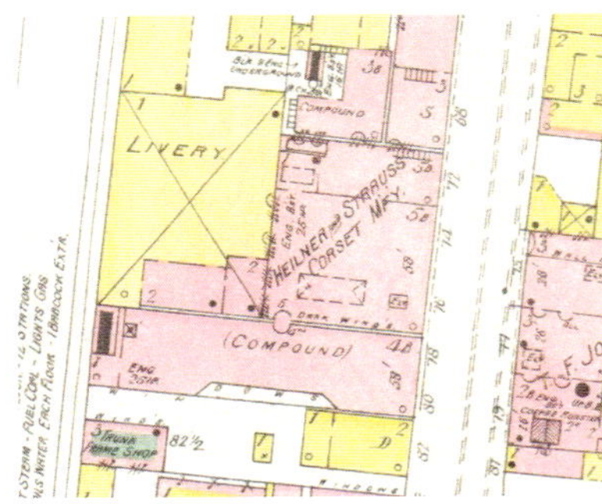

HEILNER & STRAUSS CORSET MANUFACTURING COMPANY

JACKSON AWNING COMPANY
FOUNDED 1878
186 MARKET ST

NEWARK EMBROIDERY WORKS
FOUNDED 1881
78-84 SHIPMAN ST

NICOLAS ZNEIMER BUTTON WORKS
166-174 NJ RAILROAD AVE

BASCH & GREENFIELD
28-46 SUMMER AVE, 59-67 7TH AVE,
58 CRANE ST

CONMAR ZIPPER COMPANY
140 THOMAS ST

COOPER SPORTSWEAR
MANUFACTURING COMPANY
BUILT 1920
720 FRELINGHUYSEN AVE

IMPERIAL LAUNDRY COMPANY
FOUNDED 1903

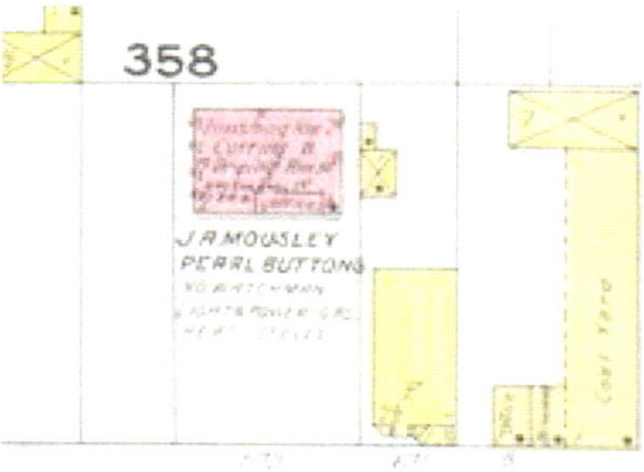

J.A. MOUSLEY PEARL BUTTONS
673 S 16TH ST

JABURG & BERNHARD
FOUNDED 1912, BUILT 1878
418 CENTRAL AVE

SINGER MANUFACTURING
COMPANY SILK MILL
236-248 BANK ST

STOUTENBURGH & COMPANY
799-805 BROAD ST

WEINGARTEN'S CORSET
FACTORY
401 HIGH ST

THE CRUCIBLE STEEL COMPANY OF AMERICA

Crucible Steel Company factory, c. 1920

The Crucible Steel Company of America is a major manufacturing company that was formerly located in Harrison, N.J. A collective group of companies using a similar production method joined forces to bolster their efficiency and started operations in Harrison as Atha Works.

In 1900, the company produced metal and steel, but the beginning of World War I prompted them to produce and research their methods for alternative purposes for the war effort. This included bulletproof steel for men operating field artillery that previously protected bank vehicles, or Chrome Molybdenum, which was an alloy perfected to produce airplanes, motor vehicles, and ordnance.

The factory complex included a variety of structures for different functions including a rolling mill, a forging shop, a gun barrel shop, a hydraulic plant, a turbine station, an open-hearth building, and a reservoir. Post-World War I, the company shifted its focus to locomotive repairs, until World War II, when they produced weapons and ammunition to aid in the war effort. After the war they focused on producing cold rolled steel.

The rolling mill building during demolition, 2018 (Photographs by Lucas Castellane and Kersyn Wood)

Eventually they left Harrison like most of the industry there and moved to Syracuse, N.Y. This may have been a result of Colt Industries buying the company in 1968. Other metal and plastic manufacturing companies including the Guyon Pipe Company then used the buildings.

Demolition of the factory complex began in the 1990s with the open hearth and ordnance buildings. By 2018, the rolling mill was the only remaining structure as the Red Bull Arena, a few apartment complexes, and a new commuter train station in Harrison now occupied the site. The rolling mill was a steel shed structure faced in Washburn brick that as it was dismantled, revealed the vast, interior column-free space. Students Lucas Castellane and Kersyn Wood had the opportunity to document the demolition while researching the company. It is now a parking lot.

The rolling mill building during demolition, 2018 (Photographs by Lucas Castellane and Kersyn Wood)

FACTORY PROCESS

Workers straightening and cutting drill rods, c. 1925

The Crucible Steel Company of America was formed as a collective effort of thirteen different companies, each using the specific method of steelmaking known as the Crucible Method. This method involved the use of a furnace, which held around thirty graphite crucibles and contained a surplus of iron with additional alloys.

McCoy, C. W., "Stainless Steel Manufacturing Process and Equipment." Patent 3,336,132. 15 August 1967.

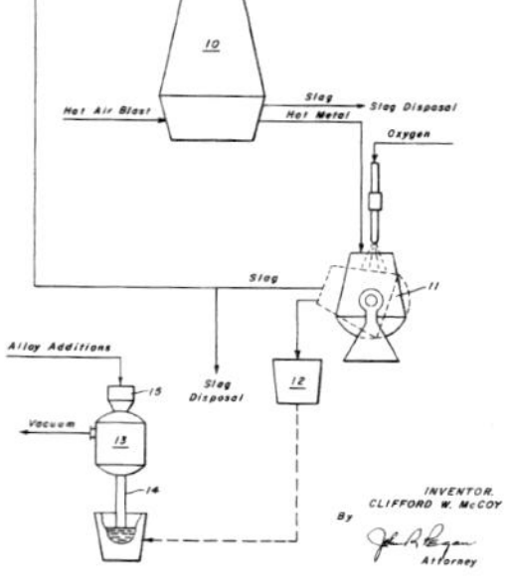

The mixture of various ores included such materials as: sintered iron ore, raw iron ore, high chromium ore, limestone, gravel, and coke which is a type of fuel with high carbon content and few impurities. These ores combined with aggregates and slag containing chromium into the furnace.

This metal would be heated until the iron and alloys became molten, at which point the crucible filled with molten steel, called a charge, would be taken from the furnace by an employee using a large set of tongs. The steel would then be teemed, which is the process of pouring the liquid steel into molds, shaped as ingots. This method, dubbed the "crucible method," was time-consuming and laborious, but produced the highest quality steel for tool production at the time, and so was deemed a necessity.

An additional stage of this process was the post-teeming cleaning of the crucibles, which would involve cleaning and leveling the bottom of each crucible by scraping away the excess metal once it had cooled. This was done because extracting excess molten metal was extremely dangerous, messy, and difficult, so the steel had to cool and be scraped away.

After this, the crucible interiors would be lined with a layer of fire clay to allow for easy removal of the molten steel. This process produced the highest quality steel for tools and became a tried and trusted method of production, aided over time by new technology which has allowed for it to produce high-quality metal made through a new method known as the Crucible Particle Metallurgy (CPM) process.

The CPM process integrated the smelting of the crucible method with new techniques for removing carbon and sulfur. The CPM process diverged from the traditional method by having the molten steel poured into a nozzle, which was atomized, or reduced into very fine particles, and sprayed and cooled to form a uniform powder. This powder was heated and poured into ingots.

The metal was then brought into a rolling process where it was either hot- or cold-rolled. This process rolled the steel at a temperature above its recrystallization point for hot rolled steel, or cold rolled by going through additional cooling processes, which toughened the steel and readied it for its final stage of milling to be formed into finished products, which were then shipped out and distributed.

LEFT:
Workers using crucible melting furnaces, c. 1925

RIGHT:
Workers use a Brinell machine to determine hardness values, c. 1925

HANOVIA CHEMICAL & MANUFACTURING COMPANY

The Hanovia Chemical & Manufacturing Company factory, 1912

The Hanovia Chemical & Manufacturing Company, once located at 235 New Jersey Railroad Avenue, still provides Ultraviolet lamps and photochemical equipment from their factory in Fairfield, N.J. Hanovia was an early developer of UV lamps and had a powerful marketing campaign for its signature product.

The company was founded in 1905 by Charles Engelhard, a "tough businessman" according to his son in a 1965 *Forbes* cover story. He established a career in precious metals with the acquisition and founding of several companies including Baker & Company, Irvington Smelting, and American Platinum Works. The Hanovia Chemical and Manufacturing Company was an interrelated addition to Newark, providing precious metals for ceramic and glass industries, UV equipment used by the dairy industry to irradiate and enrich natural milk, and fine quartz glass for scientific uses and products. Developing UV lamps for medical and therapeutic purposes became a priority for the company. In their advertisements they touted the importance of natural sunlight for health and wellness, and demonstrated how the UV rays produced by the sun were critical to good health. Their products were pushed alongside free reading material that explained ultraviolet rays and their benefits, as well as material, which marketed the luxury of the ultraviolet light-bath.

The two-story, 50,000-square-foot factory building was previously occupied by the Tomlinson Spring Company. The lamp processing used the building's verticality in maintaining a constant flow of materials in and products out of the building through its main loading dock. However, the process was hazardous as the pollution spewing from the factory's smokestack required remediation by the Newark Health Department. Additionally, there was a lawsuit between Hanovia and Westinghouse, another Newark notable manufacturer of electrical products (see page 116), regarding the development of their lamp, which Hanovia claimed was an infringement of their patent in 1948.

Though it had a relatively small operation with a payroll of about twenty workers in its early years, the company continuously developed new products as they expanded and merged with other enterprises to become an international company.

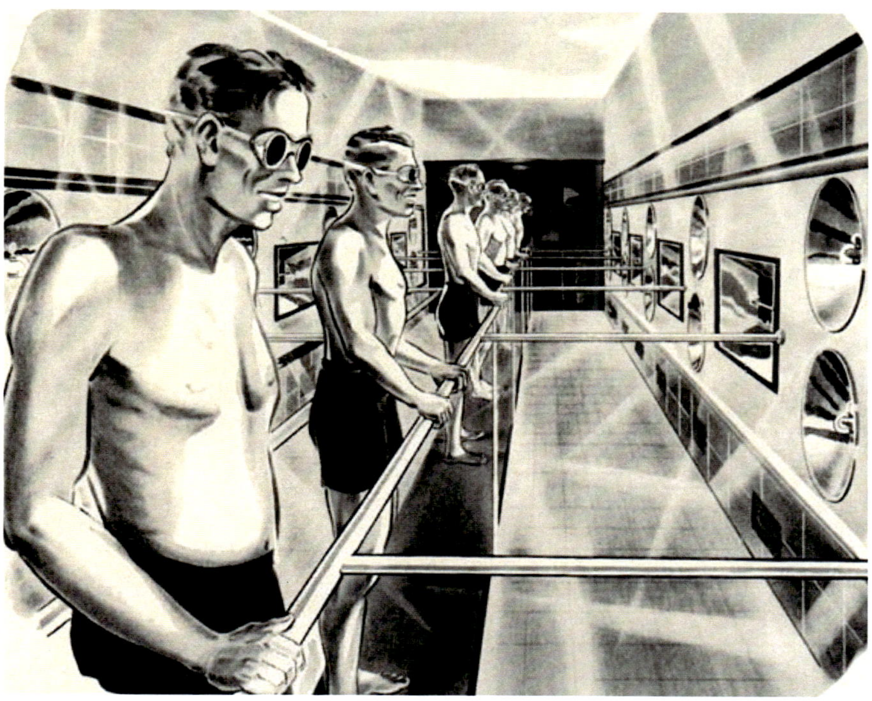

Workers increase their efficency by regularly bathing with Hanovia Ultraviolet Sun Lamps, according to an advertisement, 1942

J
K
I
D
G
B
E
F
A
H
C
A
A
ADJACENT HIGH POLLUTING
FORMER FACTORY SITES
A MURPHY VARNISH COMPANY
B HANOVIA CHEMICAL & MANUFACTURING COMPANY
C A. HOLLANDER & SON TANNERY
D KAUFHERR & COMPANY CALF LEATHERS
E FLOOD & CONKLIN VARNISH COMPANY
F THE BIGELOW VARNISH COMPANY
G F.W. DEVOE & C.T. RAYNOLDS VARNISH COMPANY
H MARK W. MAHON LEATHER COMPANY
I SEYMOUR & WHITLOCK INCORPORATED
J BLESS & DRAKE INCORPORATED
K AMERICAN PATENT LEATHER COMPANY
Google Earth
Imagery © 2021 Google, Bluesky,
Maxar Technologies, Sanborn,
USDA Farm Services Agency,
Map data © 2021 Google

CURRENT CONDITION

Site of the former factory, 2019

Following the death of Charles Engelhard, his son, Charles Jr., inherited and consolidated the family companies into Engelhard Industries in 1960. Operations had begun at a 42-acre site on Delancy Street in Newark in 1954. It's possible the factory on New Jersey Railroad Avenue ceased operations around this time. In 2006, the corporation was purchased by a German chemical manufacturer but Hanovia Specialty Lighting LLC still manufactures UV lamps, power supplies, assemblies of reflectors, and curing systems in New Jersey. They also produce photochemical equipment and custom designed systems for pharmaceutical and fine chemical industries, air/water sterilization products and photoluminescent pigment/vinyl products for safety, educational and novelty purposes.

The factory in Newark was demolished around 2000 and the site is currently vacant with the exception of an unfinished four-story apartment building. The site, 100 Chestnut Street, was identified as an active brownfield site in 1999. While Newark is working on brownfield site clean-up on riverfront industrial sites in the North Ward, the Hanovia site remains dormant unlike the nearby remediated site which is now occupied by an elementary school.

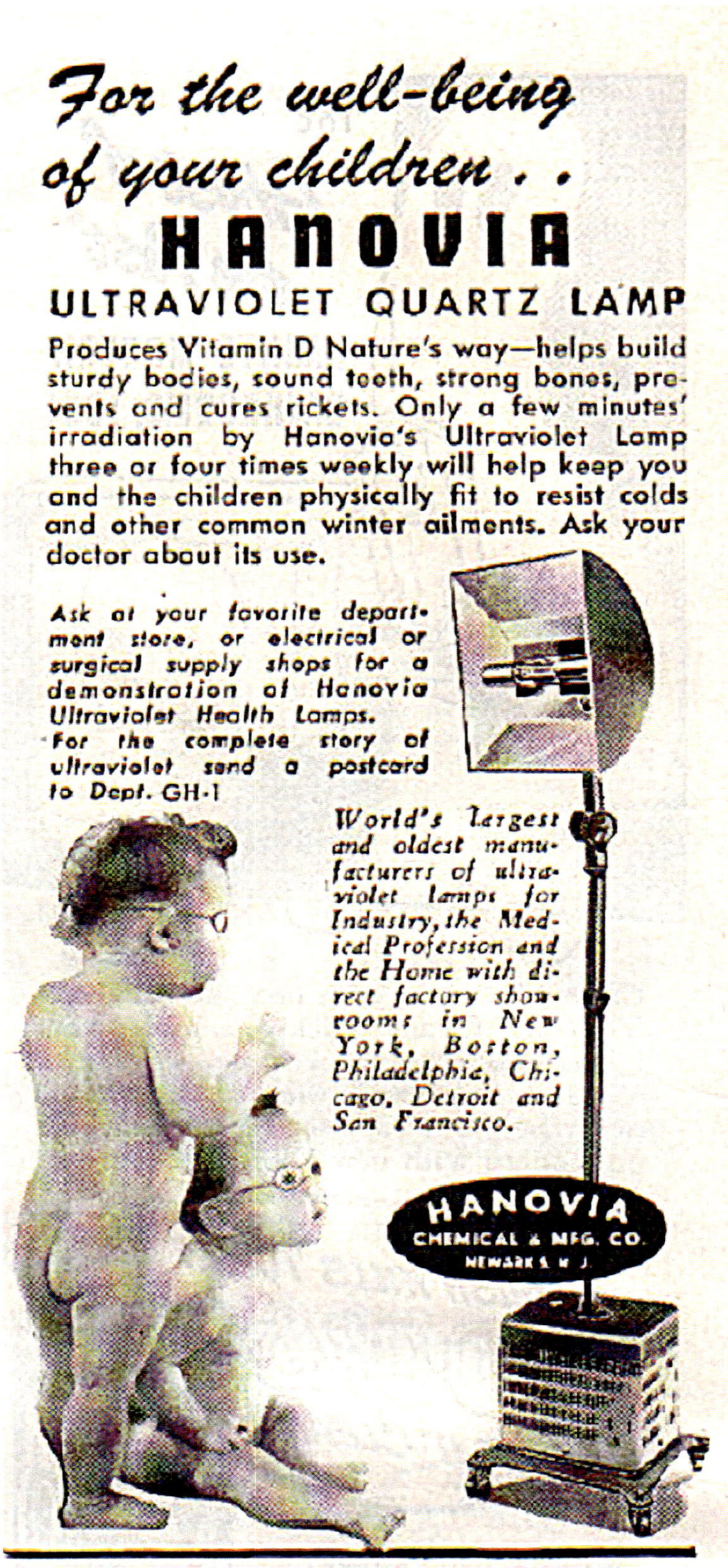
For the well-being of your children . .
HANOVIA
ULTRAVIOLET QUARTZ LAMP
Produces Vitamin D Nature's way—helps build sturdy bodies, sound teeth, strong bones, prevents and cures rickets. Only a few minutes' irradiation by Hanovia's Ultraviolet Lamp three or four times weekly will help keep you and the children physically fit to resist colds and other common winter ailments. Ask your doctor about its use.
Ask at your favorite department store, or electrical or surgical supply shops for a demonstration of Hanovia Ultraviolet Health Lamps.
For the complete story of ultraviolet send a postcard to Dept. GH-1
World's largest and oldest manufacturers of ultraviolet lamps for Industry, the Medical Profession and the Home with direct factory showrooms in New York, Boston, Philadelphia, Chicago, Detroit and San Francisco.
HANOVIA
CHEMICAL & MFG. CO.
NEWARK, N. J.

HANOVIA BEACON
CHARLES RAIMONDO

Rendering of *Hanovia Beacon*

The *Hanovia Beacon*, by student Charles Raimondo, recreates the cataclysmic presence of the Hanovia smokestack but instead uses it as a beacon of light to draw spectators to an educational and cultural attraction. A facsimile factory will also be built. The brick, one-by-six-bay structure resembles the original building on New Jersey Railroad Avenue before seven additional parcels were purchased in 1929 for $700,000 to allow the factory to expand.

The structure has a simple cornice and inset walls that will display large graphics about company information over the years, advertisements, and other brownfield remediation efforts in Newark. The Hanovia Chemical & Manufacturing Company advocated for natural sunlight for health and wellness while creating contaminated land that won't be remediated for decades. Visitors can learn about supporting brownfield cleanup in Newark or simply admire the luxury of the historic ultraviolet light-bath while standing in the sun.

OPPOSITE:
Advertisement for Hanovia Ultraviolet Quartz Lamp

JAMES A. BANISTER COMPANY

Advertisement for Banister Shoes, c. 1920

Banister & Son Company was established in 1845 by Isaac Banister, a skilled shoemaker working alongside his father. His custom shoe shop began at 114 Market Street and his son, James Banister, became a partner in 1852, forming the Isaac Banister & Son Company relocating to a larger facility at 252 Market Street. Following Isaac's retirement and the death of another business partner, Lyman S Tichenor, the company continued under the name James A. Banister Company. Shoes and other leather products were a major nineteenth-century industry in Newark because of the city's extensive leather tanneries, especially after Seth Boyden introduced patent leather in 1818.

The company moved its operations six times, often because of fire devastation, until it found its final home at 370-386 Orange Avenue, next to the Morris Canal. Frank Hill Smith, a Dayton-based engineer, known for his innovative reinforced concrete, designed the state-of-the-art fire resistant building that still stands today. It is an example of a "daylight factory," referring to early twentieth-century American industrial buildings designed to provide ample light and ventilation while maintaining open floor space. The five-story reinforced concrete building with brick walls and large steel frame windows is an "L"-shape measuring 130 by 275 feet with seven by fourteen bays. Natural light was important for the fine, detailed work of Banister shoe craftsmanship. The main structure was four stories with a basement that is revealed with the slope of the building site, and small towers at the North and South ends supply an additional floor. The boiler room/engine room was located in a separate structure that was eventually connected to the main factory building. A smokestack stood next to this one-story brick building. The factory also included a small garage and a security shed.

The company closed in 1930, leaving their building vacant for five years until the Tung-Sol Lamp Works, Inc. began using it as a radio tube factory. The Tung-Sol company was founded in Newark in 1907 and manufactured a variety of lamps and vacuum tubes. After the company was purchased by Wagner Electric in 1966, operations continued for a decade until the property was sold to Community Information Referral Services Inc. The City of Newark eventually seized the property as the result of tax lien foreclosure. The Domino Manufacturing Corporation used the factory for wrapping paper production starting in 1999. In 2015, the building was listed on the New Jersey Register of Historic Places and the U-Haul Corporation converted it into a rental storage facility.

Image of James Albert Banister and his son, Isaac, c. 1920

Illustration of the factory, 1915

FACTORY PROCESS

Isaac Banister was a traveling shoemaker, which was typical before shoe factories were made possible by industrialization. He traveled to settlements and made shoes for families—enough to last until his next visit—which traditionally entailed making shoes for the biggest member of the family and the smallest. Farmers would supply the leather by tanning their cattle and Banister would select wood from their wood pile to use as a mold. In 1845, he established his shop on Market Street that would be carried on by five generations of craftsmen.

In the early days of the company, when Isaac Banister operated this small shop, shoes were only manufactured by hand. In 1858, Lyman Reed Blake invented a machine for stitching the outsole of a shoe to the insole that was quickly bought by the engineer and businessman Gordon McKay. The Banister Company produced shoes with a handcrafted quality so that even when they introduced machinery, the workmanship had to meet a hand quality standard.

The process began with cutting and marking the leather for assembly. The pieces were then cut and hole punched. Workers sewed together the leather and the lining of the shoe applying a amount of glue to keep them in place. They then added a toe cap and a counter along the back of the heel to reinforce the shape.

Next, the material was attached to the insole of the shoe. A solid wood mold called a last was nailed to the insole to guide the leather into the required size and shape. The leather upper was stretched around the last and glued or nailed to the sole. It was kept like this for hours or days to retain the shape.

In 1878, the "Goodyear Process" replaced the step of stitching the outsole to the insole with McKay's stitching machine. This process introduced a welt which is a firm strip of leather that attached the shoe material to the sole on both sides. The welt was then attached along the bottom of the insole along the entire perimeter except for the heel and the leather, fastened directly to the insole. Additional piping was pinned beneath the heel.

With the insole completely attached, the shoe last was removed and the shoe retained its appropriate shape. The insole, however, was uneven and indented. A filler layer of cork was glued to the bottom to hold the material firmly in place. The outsole and heel were assembled and abraded to correct any imperfections in shape. Any remaining pins were removed and the shoe was finished. The company's logo was stamped on the bottom and ready for sale in stores.

OPPOSITE:
Interior views of the James A. Banister factory, 1891

The former factory, 2020

CURRENT CONDITION

The former factory entrance, 2020

The U-Haul Corporation purchased the factory in 2016 after it was nominated to the New Jersey Register of Historic Places. By that time, the building had been modified substantially, most notably the removal of original windows on the first and third floors. Concrete blocks filled the openings and the remaining windows were in disrepair. The adjacent Morris Canal was also long gone and the light rail now has a station there at Orange Street.

U-Haul saw this building as an opportunity for adaptive reuse. While it couldn't be restored to its state-of-the-art "daylight factory," repairs and restorations were made with the replacement of remaining original windows and a fresh coat of paint restoring the contrasting colors of the red concrete blocks and the beige exposed concrete structure.

The next phase of renovation saw the demolition of the smokestack and substantial repairs to the main building. Incompatible red coping now decorates the towers and additional signage now conceals some original details.

NEWARK'S SHOE INDUSTRY

A. LENZ COMPANY
314 CAMDEN ST

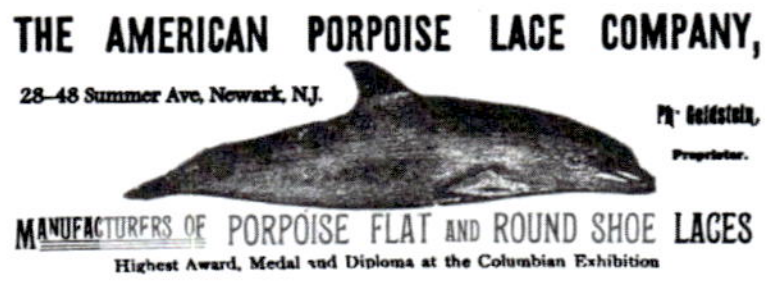

AMERICAN PORPOISE LACE COMPANY
28-48 SUMMER AVE

JOHNSTON & MURPHY SHOES
FOUNDED 1850
42-54 LINCOLN ST

MORRELL & ABBOT'S SHOES
FOUNDED 1898
229-233 CENTRAL AVE

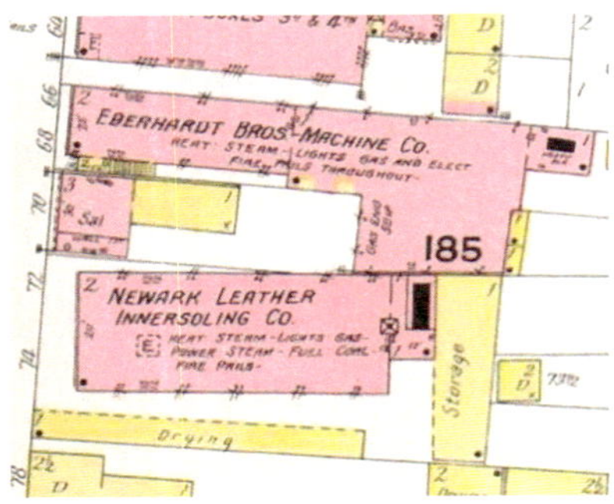

NEWARK LEATHER
INNERSOLING COMPANY

STAR HEEL PLATE COMPANY
63-81 POLK ST

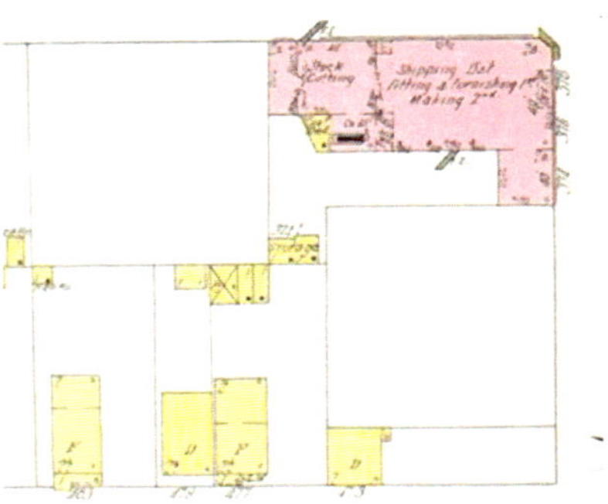

THOMAS CORT SHOE
MANUFACTORY
14TH AVE & S 20TH ST

NEWARK'S HAT INDUSTRY

C.M. HEDDEN COMPANY
FOUNDED 1899
232-242 13TH AVE

HUDSON HAT MANUFACTURING COMPANY
FOUNDED 1890
HOYT & NEW ST

J. RUMMELL COMPANY
FOUNDED 1873
PENNINGTON & DAWSON ST

M. & F. HAT COMPANY
FOUNDED 1895
58-62 COLDEN ST

MOORE & SEALY BROTHERS HAT MANUFACTURERS
121-129 NJ RAILROAD AVE

SERRATELLI HAT COMPANY
BUILT 1878
418 CENTRAL AVE

SILBERSTEIN, FLEXNER & GOTTLIEB HATS
26-32 KIPP ST
259-265 ROSE ST

W.H. MOONEY & COMPANY
216-224 HIGH ST

YATES, WHARTON & COMPANY
FOUNDED 1857
142-156 COMMERCE ST

NEWARK HAT BLOCK & MACHINE CO.
DODD, WILLIAM MANUFACTURING CO

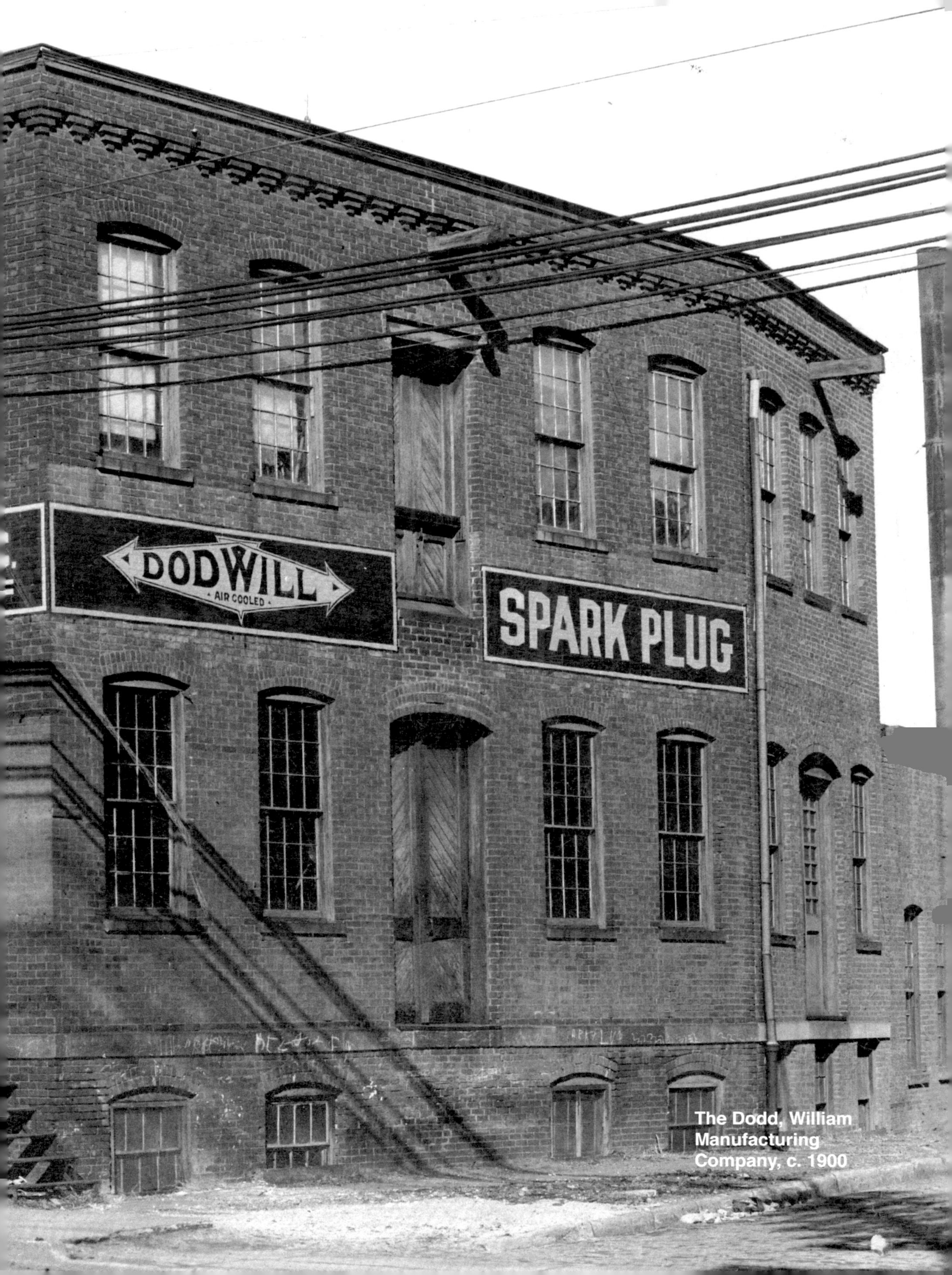

The Dodd, William Manufacturing Company, c. 1900

NEWARK'S LEATHER INDUSTRY

A. HOLLANDER & SON
FOUNDED 1889
90 POLK ST
127-159 E KINNEY ST

BLANCHARD BROTHERS & LANE
FOUNDED 1860
20 BRUEN ST

C.M. HEDDENS COMPANY
FOUNDED 1877
232-242 13TH AVE

DIEFENTHALER TANNERY
HAMILITON & BRUEN ST

ECLIPSE TANNING COMPANY
FOUNDED 1909
119 SUSSEX AVE
21 NESBITT ST

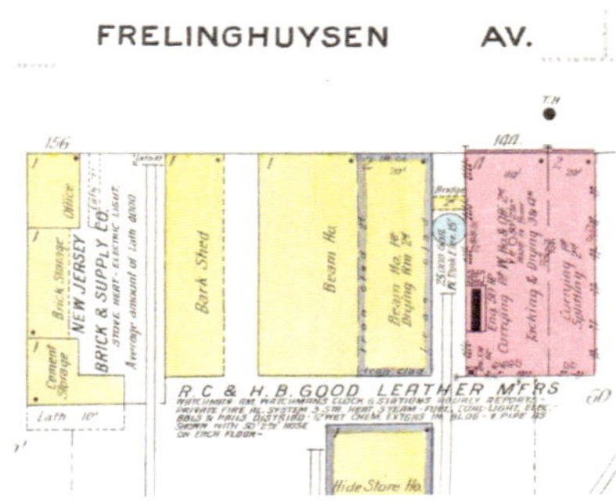

GOOD, R.C. & H.B.
FOUNDED 1894
140-150 FRELINGHUYSEN AVE

KAUFHERR & SIEGEL
FOUNDED 1908
200-204 MAGAZINE ST

MAX HERTZ COMPANY
FOUNDED 1892
54-78 OLIVER ST

OTTO OPPENHEIMER COMPANY
FOUNDED 1894
382-388 FRELINGHUYSEN AVE

CHADWICK PATENT LEATHER COMPANY
HOYT & BLEEKER ST

CHARLES HAUSELT LEATHER FACTORY
29 SPRUCE ST

COUSE & BOLTON
25-27 CANFIELD ST

HAMBURG CORDOVAN LEATHER WORKS
99-115 SUSSEX AVE
16-20 NESBITT ST

JOHN NEIDER LEATHER MANUFACTURERS

KAUFHERR & COMPANY
FOUNDED 1880
34-52 GARDEN ST
126-146 E KINNEY ST

P. REILLY & SONS PATENT ENAMELED LEATHER COMPANY
FOUNDED 1870

WARD, E.S. & COMPANY
FOUNDED 1879
414 FRELINGHUYSEN AVE

ZIEGEL, EISMAN & COMPANY
FOUNDED 1889
99 FRELINGHUYSEN AVE

Workers in the John Neider leather tannery, c. 1900

Workers endured especially toxic working conditions in leather tanneries. A newspaper article from 1933 describes the death of five men and three injured firemen after workers fell into a "waste pit" full of "deadly fumes."

MURPHY VARNISH COMPANY

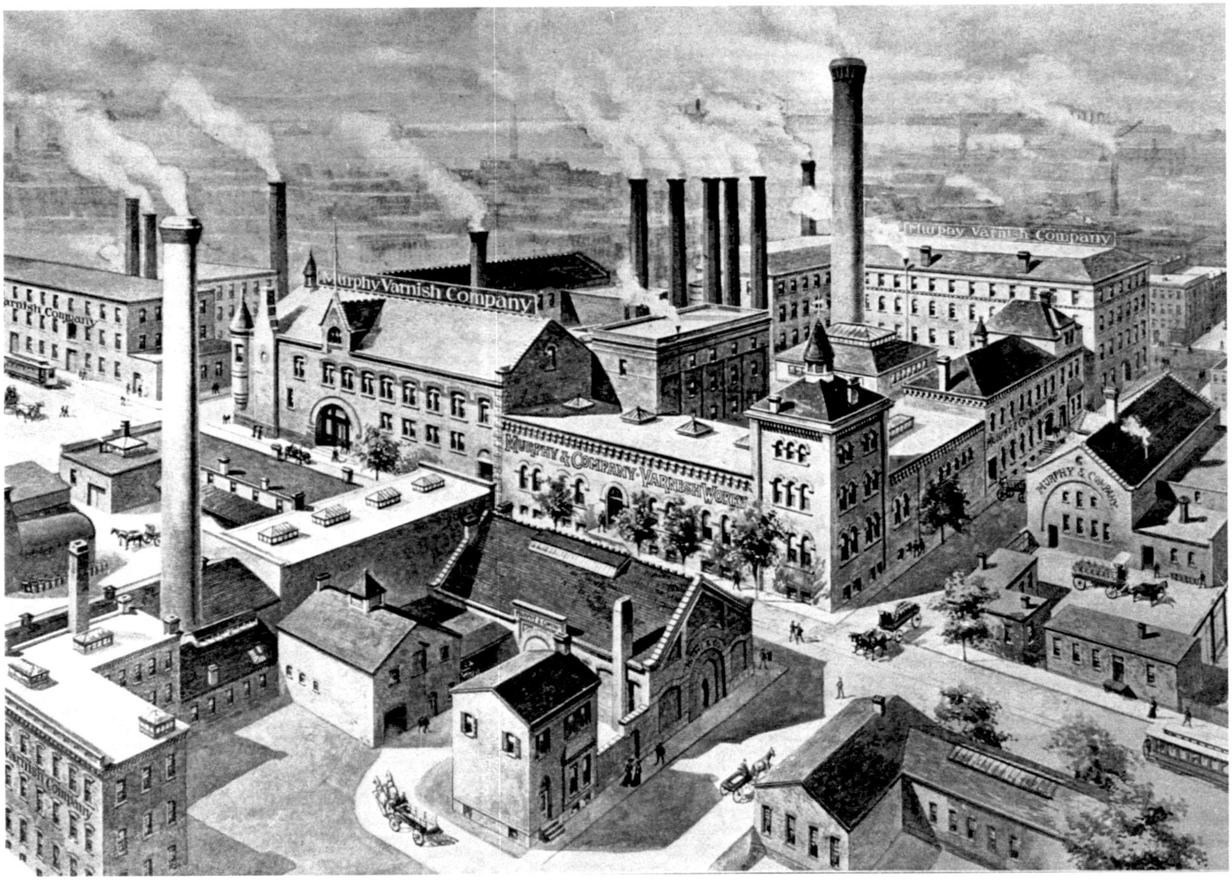

Illustration of the Murphy Varnish Company factory complex

Franklin Murphy, who founded the Murphy Varnish Company in 1865, served as the thirty-first governor of New Jersey from 1902 to 1905. The company's factory consisted of six buildings and was built in four phases between 1870 and 1905. Howard Chapman designed the central four-story building in a Richardsonian Romanesque style with a mansard roof. The steel reinforced concrete structure is seven by twelve bays with brick, sandstone, and terra cotta details. Newark-based architect James Lindsey designed smaller but more ornate additional buildings, including a two-story concrete structure in the Italianate style with a stone emblem of Murphy Varnish's trademark chariot, and a Renaissance style firehouse. Additional details included stained glass windows, most elaborate in the president's office and the large staircase window. The president's office was adorned with Roman and Venetian glass mosaics by Aeschlimann and Pellarin, and J. and R. Lamb of New York City with delicate colors and jewelled work. The staircase window included the monogram and date of establishment of the company with decorative ribbons and foliated designs. The firehouse has arched windows and a rusticated base, which is a common design throughout the factory complex.

The Murphy Varnish Company was described in *Newark: The City of Industry* as having done more than any other manufacturing industry in Newark to make the city widely known. Newark had already excelled in varnish production with large manufacturers including Flood & Conklin Varnish Works and F.W. Devoe & C.T. Raynolds Varnish Works but this was the city's largest.

Murphy Varnish became a household name by providing the finest finish products for wood, steel, and leather. Advertisements appeared in national journals and traveling salesmen routinely visited towns across the country. The company also produced a variety of household items such as calendars, postcards, and playing cards that featured signature graphics that often included the company's trademark image of the horse-drawn chariot.

The company, however, closed in 1950 due to bankruptcy. In 1979, sections of the factory complex were included in the National Register of Historic Places.

Playing card from a Murphy Varnish promotional deck of cards

FACTORY PROCESS

The four-story building designed by Chapman provided space for producing surfacers and coach varnishes with iron storage tanks in the adjacent structure designed by Lindsey according to a 1908 Sanborn Map. The Murphy Varnish Company distributed application instructions with their products called the A, B, C System. The directions corresponded to surfacers conveniently packaged in mixing cans to assist Newark's many carriage and coach manufacturers.

Varnish is produced by mixing resins, oils, and solvents. Lumber, scrap wood, and oil waste were kept in the factory complex's courtyard to be ground into resin. The raw materials were collected and dumped onto a conveyor belt to allow workers to search for imperfections in the materials such as rot from moisture accumulation. Any imperfections were discarded as the materials proceeded along the conveyor belt towards the grinding system. They were then poured into the large system of sanders and slicing units until they were ground up into a fine paste. This material was poured into rectangular containers on a conveyor belt to be processed again.

The workers then dumped the materials into into massive cooking cauldrons along with water, oils, and dissolvents. The ingredients were thoroughly mixed from 45 minutes to two hours. Once the mixing was finished, dyes were added into the liquid remains and the cauldrons were sealed and set to cook for six to eight hours at varying tempera-

Illustrations from a catalog show improvements to wood surfacer application, 1877

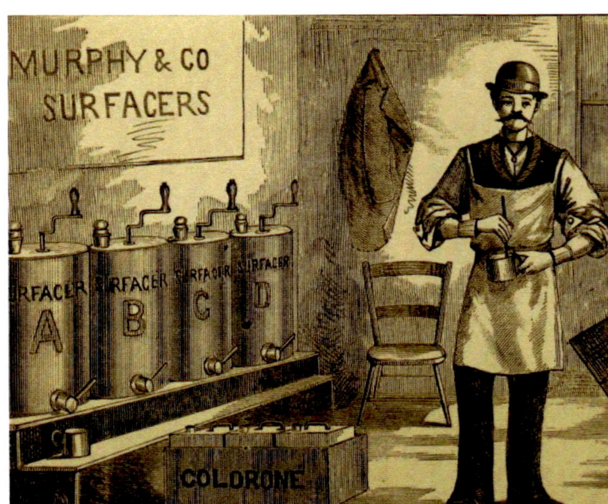

tures. Once the cooking finished, the contents were drained from the cauldrons and traveled through a network of pipes and equally distributed into canisters. The product was then tested on multiple surfaces to ensure that there were no imperfections to the batch.

Once the product passed its quality check, it was sealed and labeled. The finished product left the facility to the adjacent warehouse for storage until it was ready to be shipped out to stores.

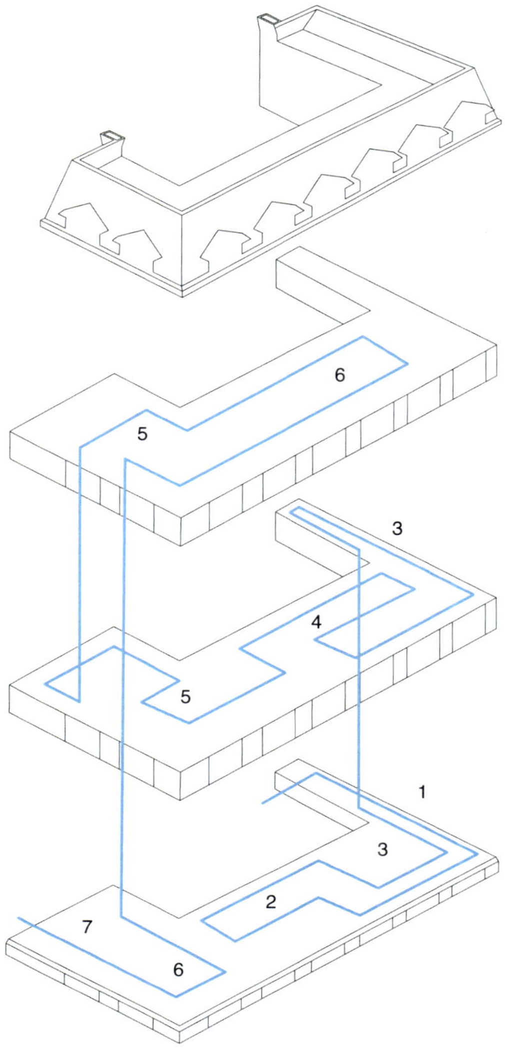

Exploded isometric factory process drawing

KEY:

1 Materials are brought in and imperfections are removed.

2 Materials are ground up into a fine pasty resin.

3 The ground-up materials are then poured into containers and pass through processing once more.

4 Materials are mixed in cauldrons and cooked.

5 The liquid is drained from the cauldrons into cannisters that are brought up to the third floor.

6 The product is quality tested on multiple surfaces. If the product passes it is then brought down to the first floor.

7 The product is packaged, sealed, and labeled. The finished product is brought out of the facility to an adjacent warehouse for storage.

CURRENT CONDITION

The former factory, 2020

OPPOSITE:
The former factory, 2020

After Murphy Varnish Company closed, the complex became a chemical storage facility. Some buildings were torn down, others left to decay. Three buildings remain today: the varnish refinery, a warehouse, and a fire station that is still used today by the Newark Fire Department. Over the years, housing developments were constructed surrounding the site and Javier Meleiro of FM Renaissance LLC purchased the remaning buildings in 2018. Studio for Urban Architecture and Design (SUAD) designed the rehabilitation of the main building into forty loft apartments and named the luxury rental building—the Murphy Varnish Lofts. Orignal materials were reused wherever possible and a seven-hundred-pound elevator wheel was repurposed in the lobby as an artwork.

A stone emblem of Murphy Varnish's trademark chariot image, 2020

MURPHY COLOR SCHEME
JAMES BRETT

Rendering of *Murphy Varnish Color Scheme*

Murphy Varnish began with the production of a few simple kinds of varnish. As production grew, the company eventually provided a list of finishing materials for anything made of wood, steel, or leather. Customers included builders and architects, railway and marine companies, and a variety of manufacturers from carriages to pianos. They produced over two hundred kinds of varnishes in about 1,200 shades of color.

The *Murphy Varnish Color Scheme*, by student James Brett, proposes coating the building today in shades of the varnish that were once produced there, making a colorful spot visible across the city. The company name would also be painted along the smokestack. The project isn't simply a vibrant paint job, its goal is to transform the factory's envelope into a memorial commemorating the founders and workers of the original complex by engraving their names into the brick exterior walls. Additionally, the sidewalks would be painted red outlining the original factory complex and acting as an interactive tour trail.

A second student project by Sean Boud features the smokestack, a remaining relic of industrial buildings that is often disregarded and demolished. His proposal *Murphy's Triumphal Column* takes inspi-

Color swatches from a company catalog stained with varnish

MURPHY'S TRIUMPHAL COLUMN

SEAN BOUD

Rendered section of *Murphy's Triumphal Column*

ration from the Romanesque style of the Murphy Varnish building and its carved emblem by applying a continuous helical frieze from the bottom to the top of the smokestack, similar to Trajan's Column. A continuous frieze will tell the story of the varnish works, the history of the building following its closure, and the role it played in the city of Newark. The top will feature a lookout platform providing a panoramic view of the city. Guests may then use an elevator to return to the ground level.

MURPHY VARNISH DESIGNS

MATTHEW SERRANO

Design for Parking Permit Tags

OPPOSITE:
Pattern Design

A third student, Matthew Serrano, focused on the Murphy Varnish Company's playing cards which had unique comical graphics depicting varnish salesmen, people worshiping cans of varnish, and showing the many uses of Murphy Varnish products. These comical graphics served as inspiration for some of the everyday elements in mixed-use communities. This project would use the Murphy graphics for such items as custom wallpaper patterns or parking permit tags for the newly renovated building complex.

NEWARK'S PAINT, INK, & VARNISH INDUSTRY

AMERICAN COLORTYPE COMPANY
BUILT 1912
659 SUMMER AVE

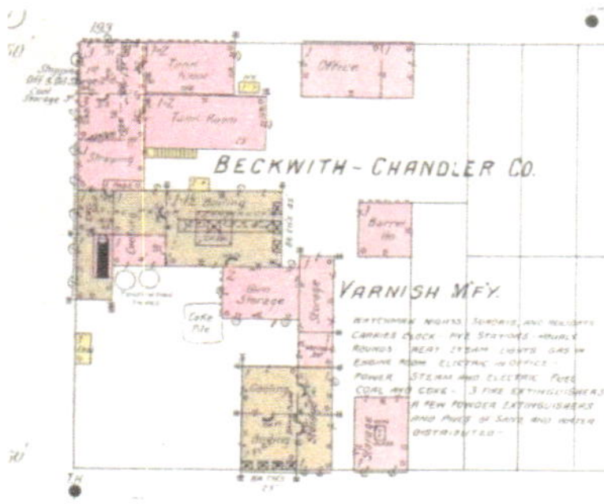

BECKWITH CHANDLER COMPANY

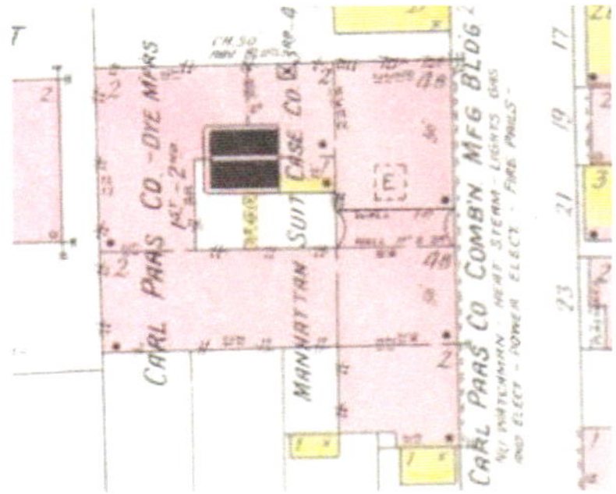

CARL PARS COMPANY

FLOOD & CONKLIN COMPANY
112-136 CHESTNUT ST

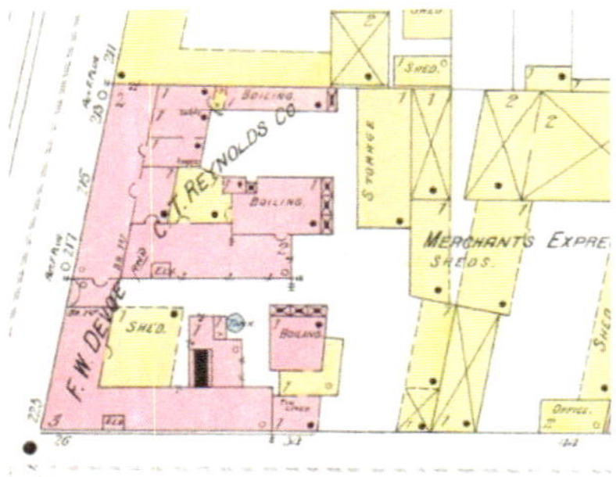

F.W. DEVOE & C.T. REYNOLDS VARNISH COMPANY
213-219 NJ RAILROAD AVE

H.W. JOHNS ASBESTOS PAINTS
4 CHESTER AVE

MAAS & WALDSTEIN COMPANY
437 RIVERSIDE AVE

MORRIS HERMANN & COMPANY
878 MT. PROSPECT AVE

PATTON'S SUN PROOF PAINTS
4 CHESTER AVE

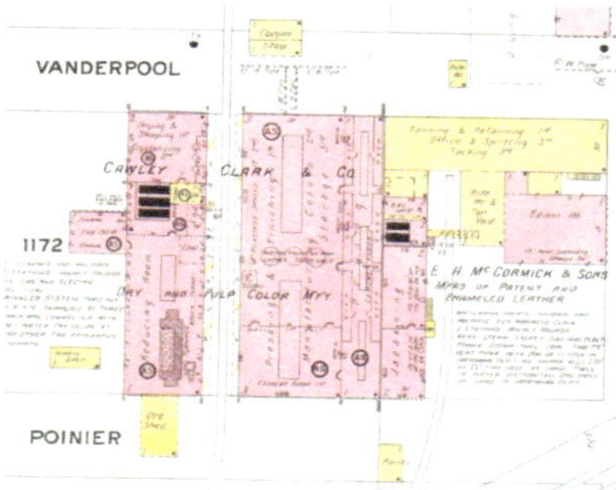

CAWLEY, CLARK & COMPANY
278 PASSAIC ST

DIXON & RIPPEL
50-52 MARKET ST

EAGLE-PICHER LEAD COMPANY
70 BLANCHARD ST

HELLER & MERZ COMPANY
FOUNDED 1869
HAMBURG PL & AVENUE M

I. POMEROY COMPANY
264 HALSEY ST

JAENECKE PRINTING INK WORKS
WRIGHT ST & AVENUE B

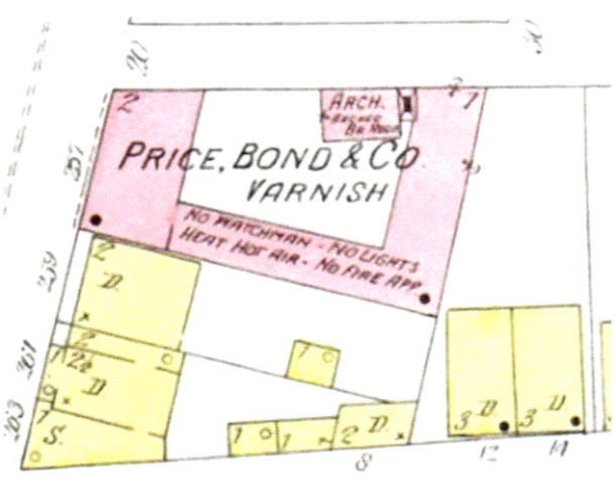

PRICE, BOND & COMPANY
NJ RAILROAD AVE & VESEY ST

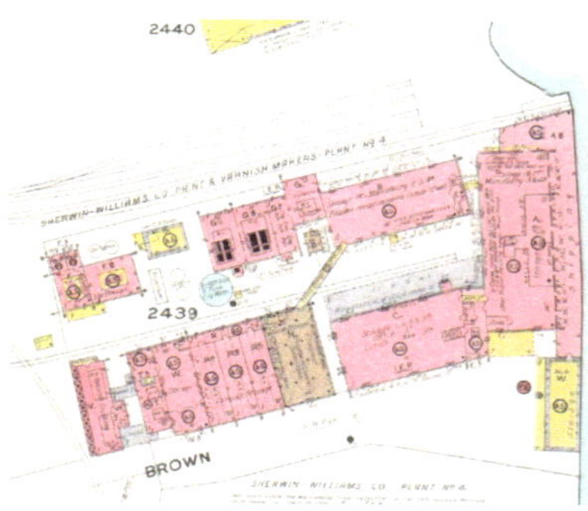

SHERWIN WILLIAMS COMPANY

WILLIAM DIXON & COMPANY
FOUNDED 1857
84-88 MECHANIC ST

SHIFMAN MATTRESS COMPANY

The Shifman Mattress Comapny factory, 2020

The vacant warehouse building, 2020

Established in 1893, the Shifman Mattress Company still operates today in their factory on Mott Street since 1918. The four-story, brick and steel frame building was formerly a part of a leather tannery complex for P. Reilly & Son whose name is still visible as a palimpsest on the Raymond Boulevard side of the Shifman building. A Sanborn Map from 1892 reveals this site previously housed a cellar for Hensler's lager beer before P. Reilly & Son expanded across Mott Street with the construction of more production space, storage space, and a large exterior drying yard. Part of the first floor was dedicated to applying a coat of oils and pigment to the hides called the daub coat. It is a thick coating that is then removed, a finish is applied, and the hides are then japanned, meaning baked and sunned. This first floor of the building had only a few small windows which have since been filled in with concrete blocks. Some of the tannery complex remains, including the abandoned brick warehouse across the street, although a steel bridge over Mott Street was removed. This part of the complex served as a factory for the Special Handle Manufacturing Company established in 1920.

Trucks at the loading dock, c. 1940s

By 1927, Shifman Mattress Company had already built an addition to their factory with a loading dock. Shifman's latest expansion was in 2008 to add a new warehouse, a larger loading dock, and alterations to manufacturing space, tripling its capacity.

In 2019, the abandoned warehouse at 648-652 Raymond Blvd. was purchased and plans for development soon followed. Inglese Architecture and Engineering, the architecture firm that teamed up with Hanini Group for Newark's newly renovated Hahne and Company Building as well as a redevelopment design for the Pabst Blue Ribbon brewery site, are proposing 120 residential units with retail space and a parking garage.

FACTORY PROCESS

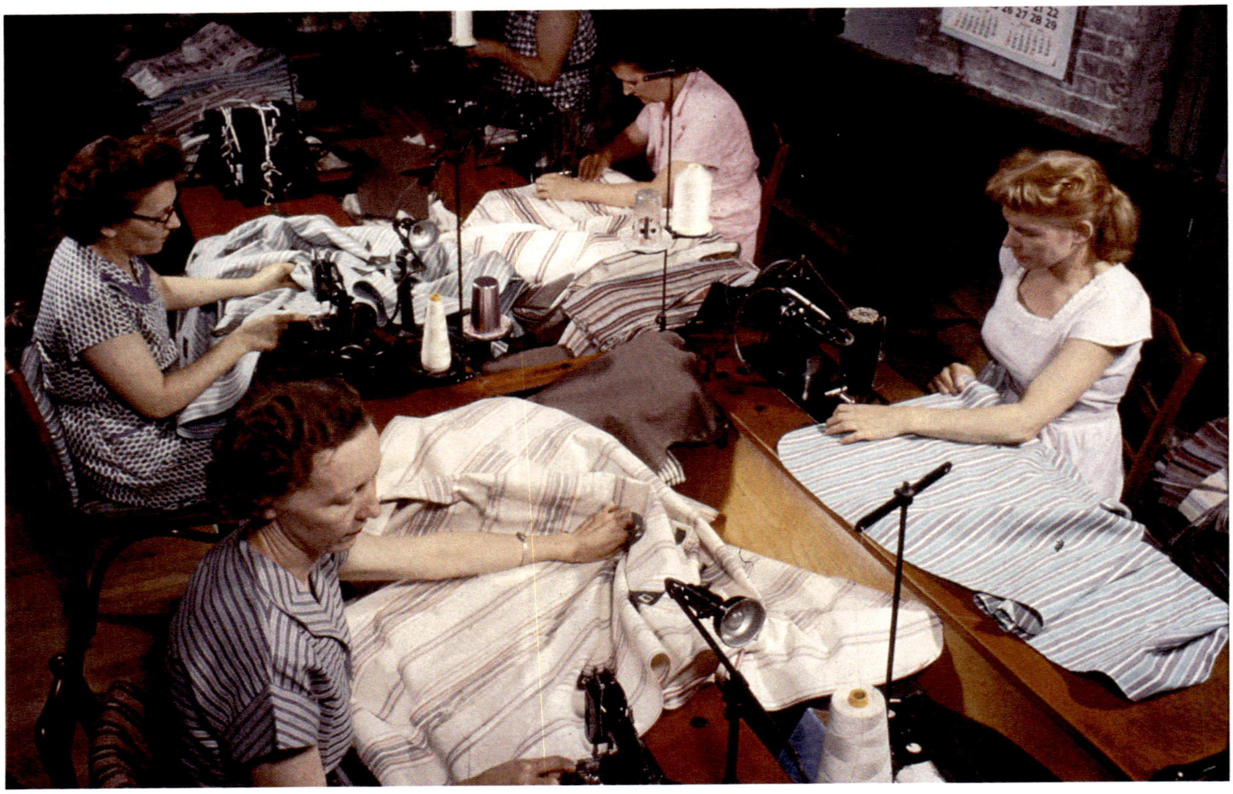

Workers sewing mattress panels, c. 1950s

Shifman continues to produce mattresses using its original techniques and traditions and the mattresses have been purchased by numerous presidential administrations including Kennedy, Clinton, and Obama. Today about 70 workers are responsible for producing Shifman's mattresses by hand. A typical mattress production requires 24 people working eight to twelve hours. Each box spring is hand tied with Shifman's signature eight-way hand tied system and the many tufted layers of fabric are sewn by hand. The original factory building is used to construct the beds while the newer addition is used for storage.

Bales of cotton weighing six to eight hundred pounds are layered into a spring box frame and then wrapped around the exterior. Shifman mattresses contain up to 83 pounds of cotton. Workers build the box frames with superior grade Canadian Spruce and recycled steel spring coils which are secured with Italian twine. Multiple layers of cotton finish the mattress and include a top panel and a side border. Workers sew together these finishing layers with a manually operated tape edge machine. They flip the mattress and the process is repeated, creating a two-sided mattress and extending its lifespan for the customer.

Workers then move the mattress to the hand-tufting area. At this stage, the mattress is about two feet thick. Workers sew the mattress to compress the layers and ensure they all stay in place. The final product is a mattress overstuffed with cotton and all-natural materials. Workers stack the completed mattresses onto dollies into the storage area where they remain until delivery to individual clients and department stores.

Worker sewing togther panels before being hand-tufted, c. 1950s

SHIFMAN SCAFFOLDING
ALEXANDER JIMENEZ

Rendering of *Shifman Scaffolding* placing production on display

OPPOSITE: Rendering of *Shifman Scaffolding*

The Shifman Mattress Company is a particularly interesting factory for an interpretive project because it is still functioning. The company has pride in their operation, sharing their techniques in magazines and allowing the occasional film crew to visit their factory.

Student Alexander Jimenez designed *Shifman Scaffolding* by stacking platforms along the building's facade on Raymond Boulevard to serve as a gallery. The faded murals on the brick wall and the lettering from the P. Reilly & Son tannery and Shifman will be restored. Additionally, informational panels will be painted within the array of windows, providing a gallery of alternating panels and views into the working factory, a seamless arrangement of old and new, static and moving, making the factory and the workers visible to the general public.

TIFFANY & CO.

The Tiffany & Co. factory, c. 1950s

In 1892, Tiffany & Co., an international jewelry company with its treasured creations and signature robin-egg-blue color, built a silver plate factory in the Forest Hill neighborhood of Newark. Newark had already established a thriving precious metals industry by then with twenty-one jewelry and fine metal-related manufacturers documented in *Newark, NJ: Illustrated*, published only one year before Tiffany began construction. Newark's silver craftsmanship reaches back as far as the 1790s with early silversmiths including Benjamin Cleveland and Epaphras Hinsdale. Larger manufacturers began competing with fine European products such as the Krementz Company who supplied products for Tiffany or the Durand Company which was featured prominently in the great 1872 Newark Industrial Exhibition. Newark also had an established engraving industry, most notably the Newark Engraving Works at Hamilton and McWhorter Streets which is now condominiums.

Tiffany & Co. had outgrown its original factory at 53 Prince Street in Manhattan and built the Newark facility for its expanding sterling silver and stationery manufacturing departments. The Romanesque-style building was designed by New York-based architects Schweitzer & Diemer as a kind of fortress to protect the precious materials inside. It was a completely self-contained process with its own source of power, steam, and water that cost a remarkable $100,000. The red brick walls are twenty-one inches thick. Brownstone was used for trim on the window sills, its four columns, and arches at the original entrance. Four linear buildings create two courtyards with two, five-story corner towers making it visible at a distance. The northern courtyard enclosed a machine building in the center while the southern courtyard remained open. An office was located in the northern tower and the southern tower held the president's office in a mahogany clad room. The main tower has a copper weathervane and formerly concealed a 20,000-gallon water tank on the fourth floor.

Vaults for gold, silver, and steel dies, designing and modeling rooms, "a library of reference work on art objects and collections of natural history objects" and "an isolated room for modeling from the nude" were included in the buildings. On the west side of the complex was the electrical plant adjacent to engine rooms and the machine shop.

Like many factories of the time, Tiffany & Co. experienced a decline in resources in Newark and eventually closed in 1984. It was added to the National Register of Historic Places in 1987.

Sanborn Map of the factory, 1931

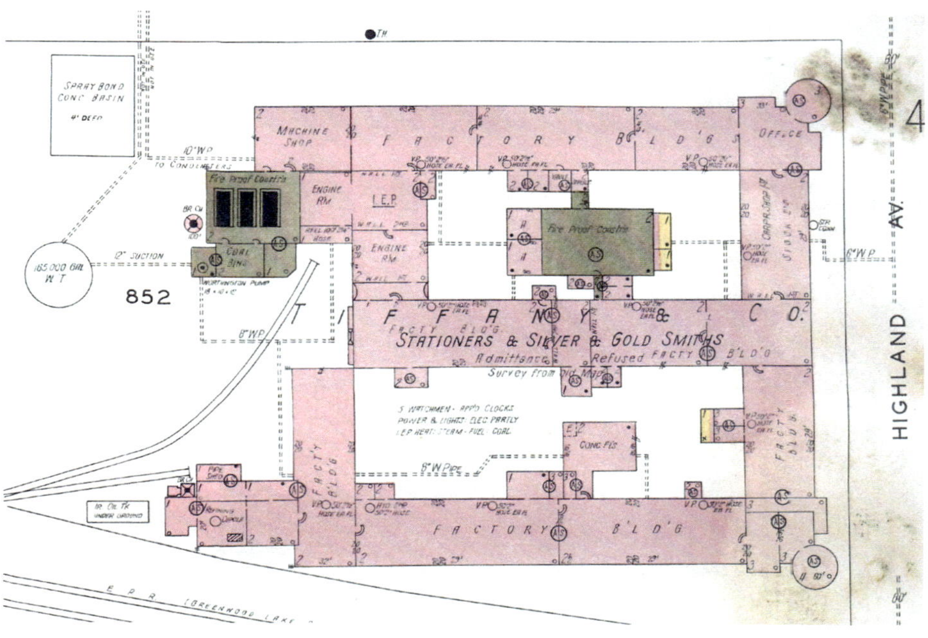

CURRENT CONDITION

The former factory along Tiffany Boulevard, 2019

OPPOSITE:
The main tower of the former factory, 2019

The Tiffany & Co. factory was converted into a gated residential community in 1993. The developer removed the northern courtyard machine building and constructed rooftop dormers for each unit. The courtyards were cleared of the accessory buildings and encroaching features of the factory. The engine room south of the machine shop, and the smokestack were also removed and the electrical plant was reduced to allow access to the northern courtyard. All residential units are entered via a gated entrance into the interior courtyard with parking.

NEWARK'S PRECIOUS METALS INDUSTRY

ART METAL WORKS
FOUNDED 1896
7-15 MULBERRY ST

AMERICAN PLATINUM WORKS
FOUNDED 1875
225-231 NJ RAILROAD AVE

BAKER AND COMPANY
FOUNDED 1904
408-414 NJ RAILROAD AVE

GEORGE HAVELL
FOUNDED 1837
284-286 WASHINGTON ST

H. G. LEFORT JEWELRY FACTORY
FOUNDED 1893
60-62 ARLINGTON ST

J.K. OSBORN MANUFACTURING COMPANY

KREMENTZ & COMPANY
FOUNDED 1866
49 CHESTNUT ST

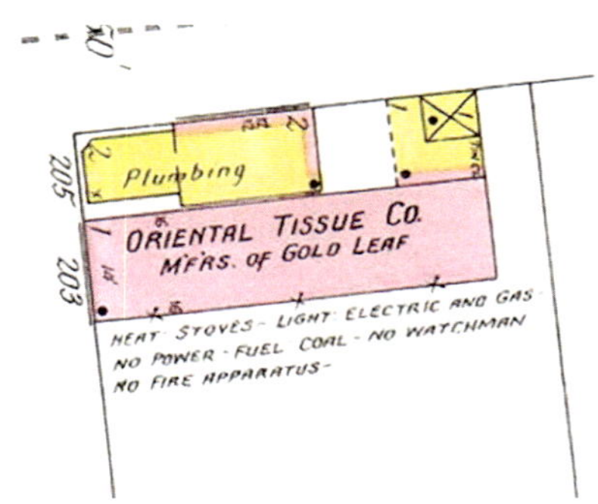

ORIENTAL TISSUE COMPANY
MCWHORTER & OLIVER ST

SHOEMAKER & PICKERING COMPANY
FOUNDED 1898
OLIVER & MCWHORTER ST

BIPPART, GRISCOM & OSBORN
FOUNDED 1886
2-8 GARDEN ST

CARTER, HOWE & COMPANY
FOUNDED 1841

DURAND & COMPANY
FOUNDED 1830
49-51 FRANKLIN ST

JOY & SELIGER COMPANY
FOUNDED 1890
53-57 NJ RAILROAD AVE

KELLER, CHARLES & COMPANY
FOUNDED 1876
213 MULBERRY ST

KERR, WILLIAM B. & COMPANY
FOUNDED 1890
HIGH & ORANGE ST

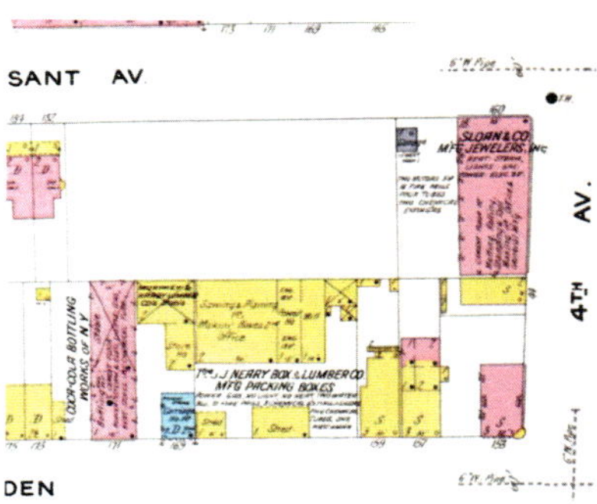

SLOAN & COMPANY
160 MT. PLEASANT AVE

UNIQUE ART MANUFACTURING COMPANY
FOUNDED 1916
200 WAVERLY AVE

WHITEHEAD & HOAG COMPANY
FOUNDED 1892
WASHINGTON & WARREN ST
SUSSEX AVE

WATTS, CAMPBELL COMPANY

The Watts, Campbell office building, 1987

Founded in 1851 as the Passaic Machine Works, the Watts, Campbell Company specialized in manufacturing Corliss steam engines. These were a major commodity to Newark industry. Steam power was ideal for manufacturing because the Passaic River could not produce enough hydropower and anthracite coal was readily available by the Morris Canal. This factory played an important role in Newark's industry by providing machinery for local clients for over 150 years such as the Ballantine Brewery, Clark Thread Mill, Murphy Varnish Company, Westinghouse, and Wiss & Sons.

In the 1880s, the factory complex consisted of approximately eleven buildings including a foundry on the Passaic River. The office building on the corner of Ogden Street (now McCarter Highway) and Mill Street is three stories tall and spans nineteen feet along the major road and extends back forty feet along Mill Street. Adjacent to this building, the blacksmith shop is a one-story brick structure with three bays that once contained a forge before being converted into an addition to the

Workers in the machine shop, 1986 reprint of a 1953 original (Photograph by Ulana D. Zakalak)

machine shop. It has a large arched entrance with batten doors and a window on either side. Decorative cast iron bosses shaped like wheels decorate the plain brick wall.

The machine shop is a cluster of buildings varying in height and surrounds the office building and extends to Passaic Street. The buildings were originally brick but the machine shop wall along McCarter Highway was stuccoed over and the slate and tin mansard roof was removed. The brick buildings have a variety of window arrangements and decorative star bolts.

The first floor contained an office, drafting rooms occupied the second floor, and the third floor was storage for patterns. The building also has a basement for valves and supply storage. The building received few alterations over the years.

FACTORY PROCESS

Workers in the machine shop, 1986 reprint of a 1953 original (Photograph by Ulana D. Zakalak)

During its successful years, the Watts, Campbell factory was bustling with over three hundred men working, horses pulling carts on rails, and large working machines. The factory equipment dated from the 1880s to 1920s and included vertical and horizontal boring mills, a wooden pivoting cantilever hoist, lathes, drill presses, grinders, planers, slotters, and jib cranes. Much of the factory work involved lifting and moving large parts into place so that a horizontal wooden bridge crane spanned the interior space with belt-driven shaft gearing on either side and a rail curved throughout the facility for the use of horse drawn carts.

In the 1920s, companies including Watts, Campbell began switching from steam to electricity. The Watts, Campbell Company received three patents for their improvements to the Corless steam engine, advertising a "30 to 2,000 horsepower" improvement on 1880s company letterhead. It was the first builders to keep the exhaust system separate from the walls of the cylinder. This reduced condensation and allowed the engine to operate more efficiently. It also invented the "dash-pot" which acted as a shock absorber for the valve. This lengthened the life of the valve and allowed it to be closed quickly without a loud noise. Other improvements included a unique cross-head with removable shoes, tapered cross-head pin and piston rod secured by a cross-key, improved piston and piston packing, a ball-and-socket bearing for the "dash-pot" plunger, and safer balance, belt and rope wheels.

Shipping and receiving moved through a large overhead door on the two-story machine shop structure along Passaic Street. South of this, there was a batten door with a hoistway door located above it for pulleys.

Workers in the machine shop, 1986 reprint of a 1953 original (Photograph by Ulana D. Zakalak)

CURRENT CONDITION

The Watts, Campbell office building, 2020

The buildings along the river were sold in 1938 as business declined. The company suffered as industry moved outside of Newark and resources and clients dwindled. The factory in Newark managed to survive longer than most, earning recognition from the National Register of Historic Places in 1986, but operation ended in 2007.

Today, the office building and the machine shop remain unused and in a state of disrepair. Graffiti covers the walls at street level and the brick shows severe erosion, especially on the two-story machine shop building along Passaic Street.

Many of the company's original machinery remains in the building, exposed to decay from the roof damage left from Hurricane Sandy. Luckily, original drawings have been preserved and are displayed in the Henry Ford Museum in Dearborn, M.I. The office interior still has remnants of its tongue-and-groove wood wainscot, chair rail, elaborate door and window moldings, and pieces of original office furniture.

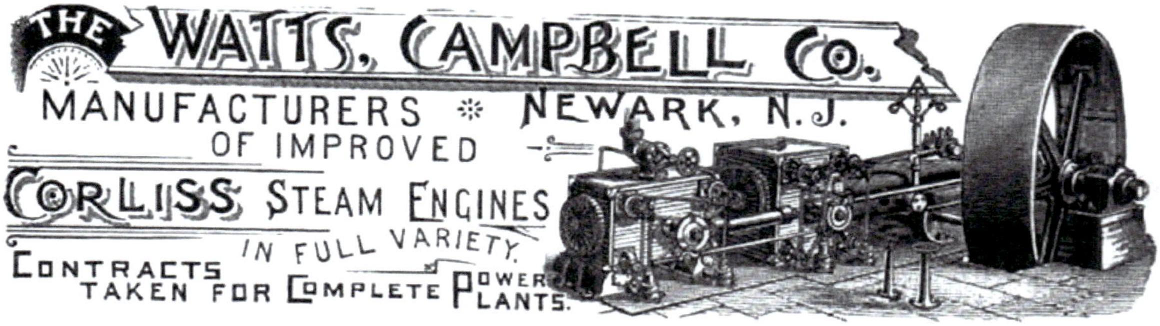

Corliss steam engine print advertisement

The current owner, the great grandson of a founder and a former employee that joined the company after serving in World War II, has been working to preserve the building and its machinery. Following its closure, the site was divided up among separate owners and the city of Newark foreclosed on it for unpaid taxes.

The former blacksmith shop, 2020

WATTS, CAMPBELL MURAL

ANDREW ENGELHARDT

Rendering of *Watts, Campbell Mural*

The contributions of Watts, Campbell Company and the reliability of their machines that gave power to several Newark manufacturers remains inside the former factory. Unfortunately, these artifacts are hidden behind inconspicuous, opaque walls that are showing signs of serious decay. The building received a partial coat of paint in 2020 but graffiti and deterioration continue to degrade the building's monolithic facade along McCarter Highway. How can the labor and machine power of this former factory become visible again without compromising the safety of these artifacts?

Watts, Campbell Mural proposes utilizing the building's blank walls as a canvas for recreating revolutionary machine renderings published in trade journals such as *American Machinist* and *Scientific American* that declared the industrial ingenuity of Newark.

Rendering of Watts, Campbell's Corliss steam engine from *the Practical Steam Engineer's Guide*, 1890

NEWARK'S MACHINERY INDUSTRY

ALEXANDER TRAUD MACHINE WORKS
FOUNDED 1876

AUTOMATIC WEIGHING MACHINE COMPANY
FOUNDED 1901
134-140 COMMERCE ST

CHARLES BURROUGHS
FOUNDED IN 1875
141-149 COMMERCE ST

GEORGE A OHL & COMPANY
157-161 ORATON ST

H.T. CLAWSON AUTOMATIC WEIGHING MACHINES
21 HACKETT ST

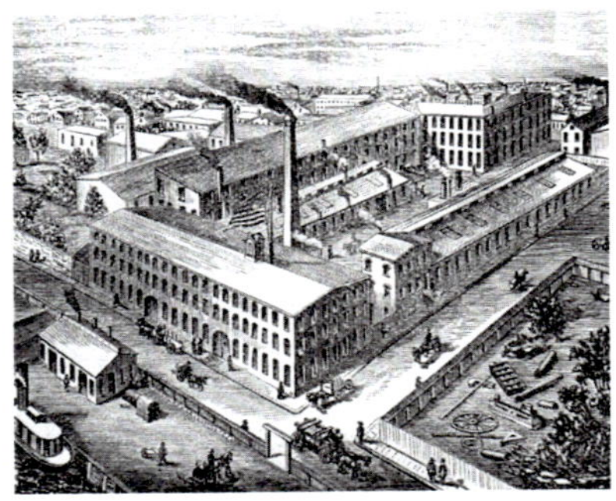

HEWES & PHILLIPS IRON WORKS

MAHER & FLOCKHART
FOUNDED 1882
MERCHANT & VAN BUREN ST

NATIONAL LOCK WASHER COMPANY
FOUNDED 1886

NEWARK GEAR CUTTING COMPANY
69 PROSPECT ST

DIXON CASCADE PUMP COMPANY
FOUNDED 1911

EDMUND JOST'S MACHINE SHOP AND FOUNDRY
FOUNDED IN 1870
350-352 PLANE ST

FREDERICK MULLER
FOUNDED 1863
214 LACKAWANNA AVE

HYATT ROLLER BEARING COMPANY
700 FRANK E. RODGERS BLVD S

JOSEPH S. MUNDY ENGINE WORKS

L.J. LYONS & COMPANY

NEWARK LEATHER MACHINERY COMPANY
125-135 NJ RAILROAD AVE

POSITIVE LOCK WASHER COMPANY
FOUNDED 1890
181 MILLER ST

STORM MANUFACTURING COMPANY
FOUNDED 1890
50 VESEY ST

Recreation period for the workers at the Hyatt Roller Bearing Company, 1916

WESTINGHOUSE ELECTRIC COMPANY

The Westinghouse Electric Company factory at the corner of Orange and Plane Streets

George Westinghouse founded the Westinghouse Electric Company in 1886 in Pittsburgh. Westinghouse was a revolutionary inventor in railroads, and patents for products including some for other manufacturers such as the Westinghouse Air Brake Company and Union Switch and Signal Company. Two years into operation, Nikola Tesla received a patent for the first alternating current motor and began working for Westinghouse Electric Company. George Westinghouse owned a lamp factory in Bloomfield, N.J., when he purchased a Newark factory in 1891 at the corner of Orange Street and Plane Street (now University Avenue). The building, completed around 1884, was adjacent to the Weston factory, which was previously the U.S. Lighting Company.

The company made several historic inventions such as building the world's first industrial air-conditioning system. It also furnished the lighting for the Chicago World's Fair in 1853 with AC power, an opportunity in which Westinghouse beat out Thomas Edison, an industry rival. In 1914, the company entered the home appliance market after acquiring Copeman Electric Stove Company. That same year George Westinghouse died leaving behind a legacy of over three hundred patents and 60 companies. By this time, the Newark factory had grown to the size of two city blocks and was referred to as the Newark Works.

It had more than 300,000 square feet of production space with 1,400 employees in its maturity. Major renovations were completed in 1904, 1911, and again in the 1950s.

The Newark Works expanded to include 80 separate buildings, with previous occupants including the Lauter Company piano factory, the Canniff Coal Company, and the First Ward Republican Club. Another building belonged to the Lansden Company, an early competitor in the electric vehicle market, which was sold by Edison after the company was left to him by the founder who began working for General Motors in 1911.

Despite its amalgamation of several buildings, the Westinghouse factory maintained a relatively uniform appearance resulting from its addition and renovation in 1904. It is a brick masonry construction with evenly spaced arched windows and a decorative brick cornice. In 1911, the two adjacent factories were added and a new building was constructed on the Southwest corner. Another addition to the factory complex was an illuminated, wall-mounted Westinghouse sign as a beacon for the company, on Orange Street with a matching sign over an entrance on the Northeast corner.

In addition to producing lighting and electrical measuring devices, the factory also made auto-ignition devices and household appliances such as heaters, toasters, irons, and radios. The first motors for electric fans were also made here. It also established a radio station. Later, the company concentrated on meters and relays. Gears, pinions, and switchboard motors were also produced for radio broadcasting and for ships.

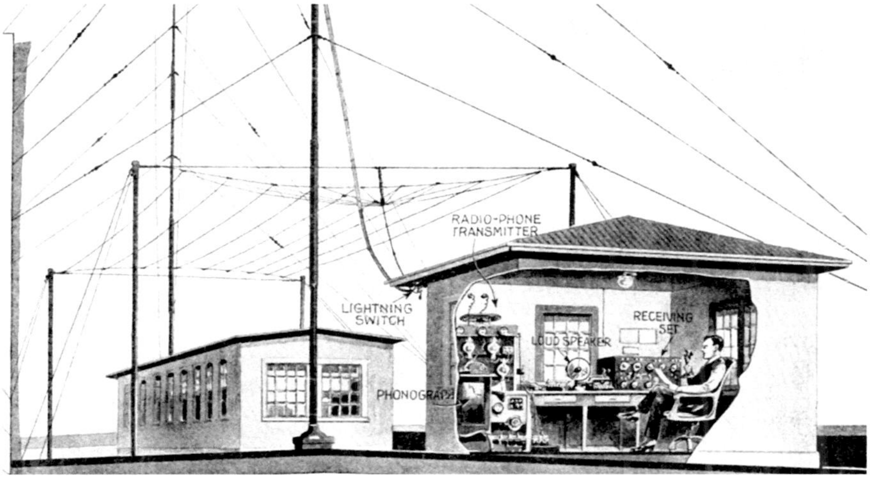

An illustrated diagram of the WJZ rooftop broadcasting station, *Scientific American*, 1922

The factory site in 2004, 2012, 2014, 2020, Google Earth

Imagery © 2021 Google, Bluesky, Maxar Technologies, Sanborn, USDA Farm Services Agency, Map data © 2021 Google

CURRENT CONDITION

The former factory site at the corner of Orange and Plane Streets, 2020

Newark Works reached a workforce of nearly 3,000 skilled female employees in 1929, but this was significantly reduced during the Great Depression. Renamed the Westinghouse Electric Corporation in 1945, production slowed down and businesses began moving out of Newark after the Newark Riots of 1967.

Westinghouse began investing heavily in manufacturing facilities in Florida in the 1970s. This was the peak of the United States nuclear power industry and Westinghouse wanted a leading role. Facilities were established in Jacksonville, Tampa, and Pensacola to build nuclear power plant components. Many of the employees of Newark Works were relocated to these facilities and the Newark factory closed in 1983.

The massive factory complex was left to decay. Parts of it served as storage for an architectural salvage company and New Jersey Transit, which operates the adjacent Broad Street light rail station. It was ultimately deemed unsafe for occupancy after concerns of toxic contamination. The Newark Works was demolished in phases beginning in November of 2007. Since then, the land has sat vacant, overgrown behind a chain link fence, with conversations of development coming and going without gaining any traction.

The most recent possibility of development is a mixed-use tower proposed in 2018 by SJP Properties and Aetna Realty. While the project hasn't been decided on yet, a rendering of the proposed structure has been published and Newark Mayor Ras Baracka has expressed interest in creating this 'transit village'.

The Westinghouse Factory

WESTINGHOUSE OUTDOOR EXHIBIT
ELIJAH WAGNER

Proposed display locations on the former factory site
Google Earth
Imagery © 2021 Google, Bluesky, Maxar Technologies, Sanborn, USDA Farm Services Agency,
Map data © 2021 Google

Elijah Wagner imagined the *Westinghouse Outdoor Exhibit*, installing informative displays on the perimeter of the site. The displays will document the many transformations of the Westinghouse factory over the past century. Each display features a case on a stand at eye level at a different period, following the long process of Westinghouse's initial factory expanding to eventually cover over four and a half acres, the subsequent uses of the building following the company's relocation, and how it ended up as an empty lot. The displays will also feature artifacts such as radios, electric fans, and electrical measuring devices to document the products and processes that were once created there.

Westinghouse did not only reach households with their products and appliances. In 1921, Westinghouse established the country's second licensed radio station broadcasting from Newark Works. The studio was on the first floor with a broadcasting station located in a shack on the factory roof. The operator here would communicate with the announcer in the studio via an intercommunicating telephone system. The station's call letters were WJZ, referring to New Jersey, and made broadcasting history by providing updated reports of the World Series game between the New York Yankees and New York Giants over the airwaves. WJZ also installed the first on-air "kill switch" after a performer referenced her support of birth control in a Mother Goose rhyme. The station was sold to the Radio Corporation of America in 1923, and moved to New York City to have access to more talent and resources. The call letters were changed to WABC.

A keychain design for sale commemorates Westinghouse products by resembling the AM Radio Model H130 from 1946.

OPPOSITE:
Display rendering for *Westinghouse Outdoor Exhibit*

BELOW:
A Westinghouse AM Radio Model H130

Commemorative keychain design

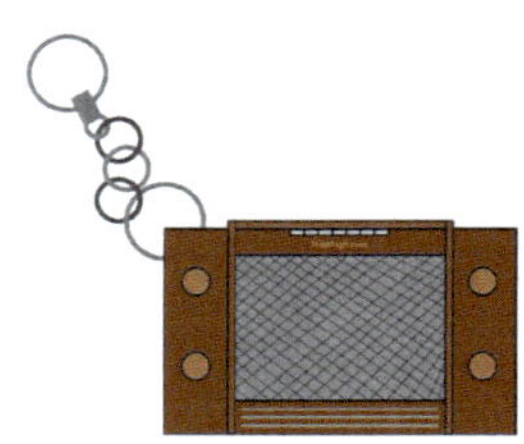

WESTINGHOUSE MEMORIAL GARDEN

DAIJA FORD

Westinghouse Memorial Garden rendered plan

Daija Ford's proposal seeks to maintain the openness of the current site by creating a commemorative garden. In a dense city environment, the nearly 150,000 square feet of open space left by the Westinghouse factory is an ample opportunity to create public green space. The space would be a calming environment for nearby businesses and universities.

The garden uses Westinghouse's 1960 logo to provide a walkway guided by topiaries. The minimalist logo was designed by Paul Rand with the understanding that a logo can only survive if "it is designed with the utmost simplicity and restraint." This design proved ageless by remaining until the end of the company, and now serves to continue its legacy.

Workers in the assembly room of the Westinghouse factory

The three anchor points of the "W" contain benches along with informational plaques recalling the patents, manufacturing processes, and the many products of the Westinghouse Corporation, capturing the revolutionary developments that occurred in Newark. Bronze replicas can also be placed in these pockets, like the many industrial artifacts that were discovered on site during demolition. The final piece, an underscore to the "W," takes shape as a reflecting pond enclosed by a small retaining wall. While George Westinghouse is memorialized with a bronze monument in Pittsburgh's Schenley Park, the *Westinghouse Memorial Garden* commemorates the workers of the Newark Works by proposing a bronze sculpture here.

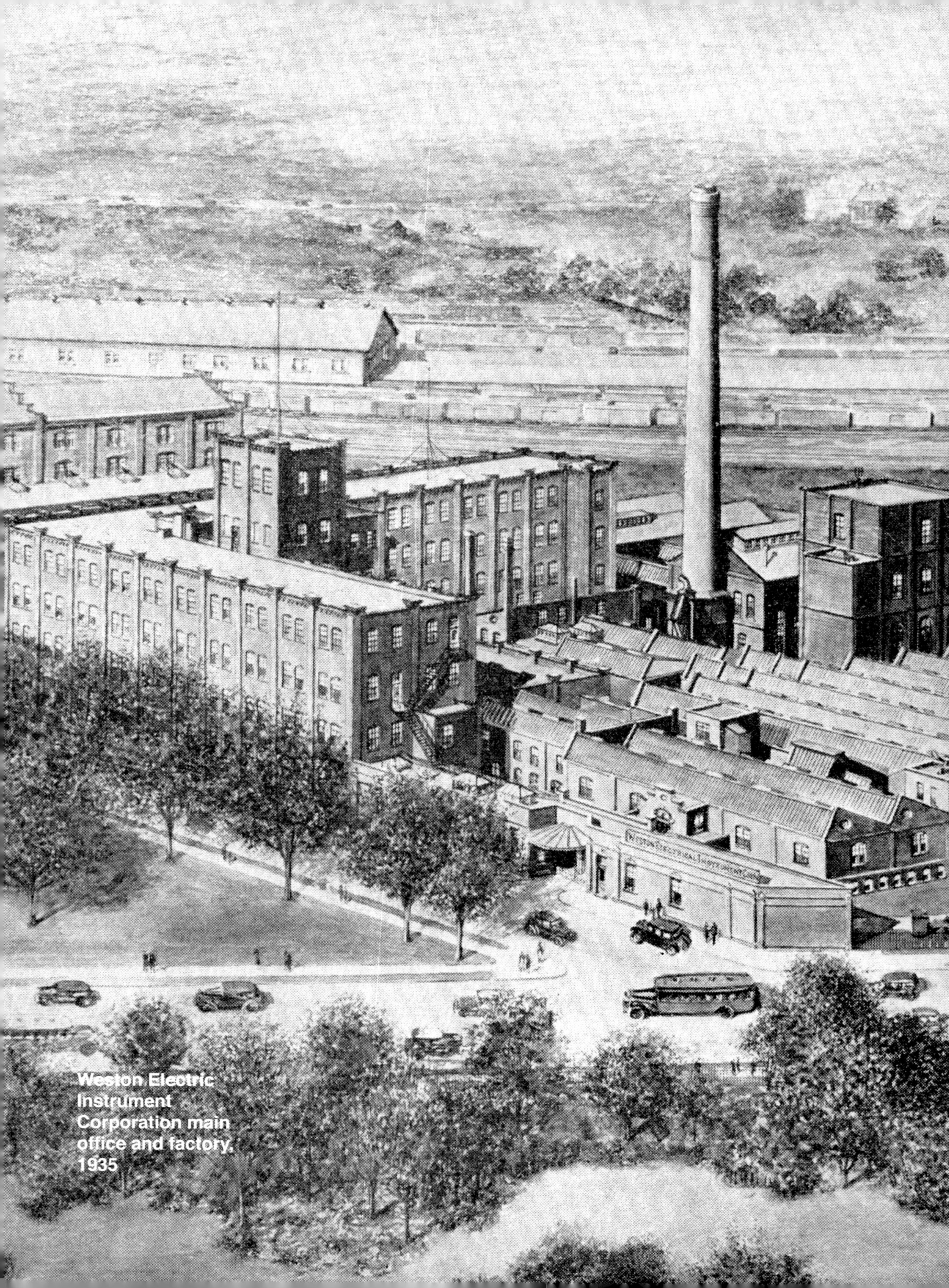

Weston Electric Instrument Corporation main office and factory, 1935

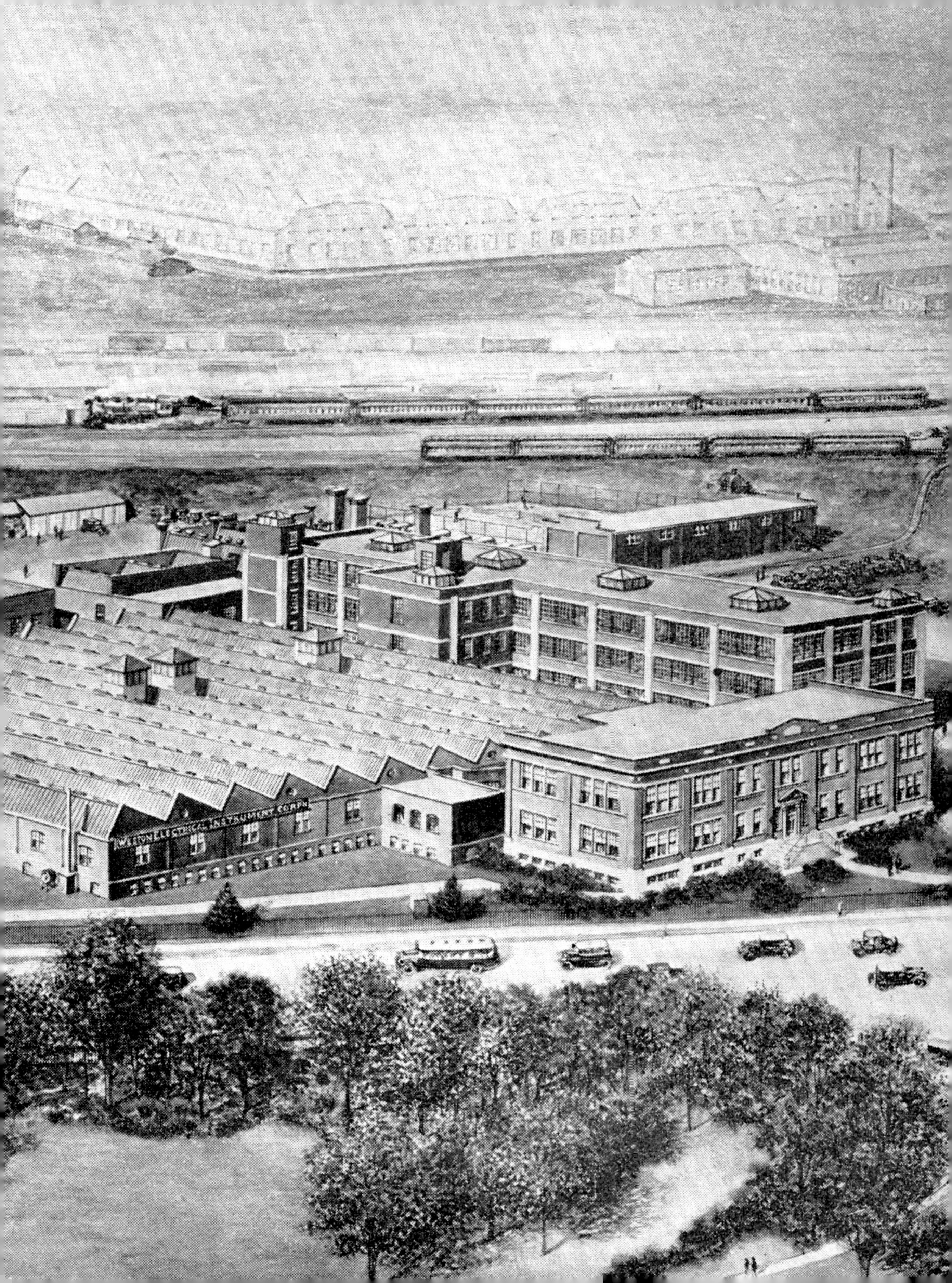
WESTON ELECTRICAL INSTRUMENT CORP'N

WISS & SONS COMPANY

Illustration of the Wiss & Sons factory, 1919

Wiss & Sons Company was a prominent cutlery manufacturer that started in 1847 when Jacob Wiss, an immigrant from Switzerland, opened a small shop at 7 Bank Street in Newark. He forged surgical instruments and shears that received worldwide recognition during the Civil War and both World Wars. As business grew and the company changed locations to accommodate production, the company opened its largest factory in 1887. It was a three-story, 40-by-200-foot masonry and timber frame building. It was located at 33 Littleton Ave but eventually grew to cover a majority of the block. An additional wing was built in 1894, adding a 35-by-160-foot production space for two hundred more skilled workers.

Factory growth diagram, 1873, 1889, 1926, 1926

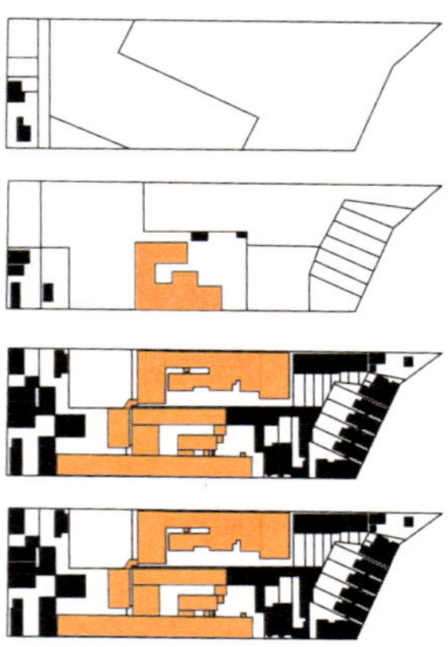

The factory relied on the Morris Canal for steel from the Rockaway Rolling Mill, in Rockaway, N.J., and coal from Pennsylvania. This factory was less than a mile from the canal and was outside of Newark's tolled lock (today's Warren Street light rail station on Lock Street) avoiding fees for barge shipments.

Wiss & Sons purchased a competitor and former employer of Jacob Wiss—Heinisch's Sons Company in 1914, making it the largest producer of fine scissors and shears in the world. Heinisch's operations moved to a factory adjacent to the Wiss factory. This building on South 6th Street was formerly the Valley Forge Cutlery Company.

The factory was modernized and expanded in the late 1960s, adding three new buildings that cost a total of $1.1 million. Additional facilities were provided for warehousing, heat-treating, and drill press

The renovated factory, c. 1976

and grinding operations, while offices were moved from the existing main plant to a "handsome modern building" as part of the "new look of Wiss" according to company literature. The company president at the time, Richard R Wiss, noted: "We again reaffirm our confidence in the future of Newark and its vitality as a manufacturing and transportation center, to serve our national and world-wide markets."

The original five-story brick building was no longer recognizable after this; a new curtain wall with fixed windows was applied to the exterior. The new panel system was flush with the building's brick cornice and left portions visible. The panels were light in color with Wiss branding in some places. Later, the building was painted coral by the Victory Temple National Holiness Church and the Boys and Girls Club of Newark who moved there in 1988. Ceramic tiles were also added to cover additional exposed brick.

The PSEG switching station in 2019
Google Earth
Imagery © 2021 Google, Bluesky, Maxar Technologies, Sanborn, USDA Farm Services Agency, Map data © 2021 Google

FACTORY PROCESS

Wiss & Sons manufactured shears that were "practically unbreakable" after improving a process designed by Seth Boyden. This new "steelforged" process replaced malleable iron with special forging steel and a high carbon crucible steel. The result was a stronger shear with a lasting cut quality and a nicer, polished finish. The process required hand precision among over five hundred operations.

The process began with a steelforged frame, which was pliable in this first stage to be corrected and shaped for comfortable handles. The cutting surface was then applied by welding a piece of steel prepared in a crucible to the frame and forging these materials together. The shear blades were warped and misshapen from this process. Excess material was cut away and screw holes drilled in. This was a very important operation that had to be correct to the one thousandth of an inch.

Next, the metal needed to be hardened. Each blade was heated to a specific temperature and immediately submerged in fresh water. Again, the blades are misshapen from this process and must be

Illustration of shears in process, 1912

Illustration of the steelforged department, 1912

STEELFORGED DEPARTMENT

Wiss & Son's factory worker

corrected. They were placed on an anvil and carefully tapped with a hammer until they were the appropriate shape, a process called peening.

Workers in the Grinding Room, which had grinding stones that vary from fifteen inches in diameter to six feet, took the crude and unfinished finished blades and corrected them. When Jacob Wiss operated his shop on Bank Street, this grinding wheel was powered by two dogs on a treadmill!

The blades were then screwed together and became a pair of shears ready for finishing. Expert shear finishers tested the quality and any shears with blades that did not meet with a perfect straight line were refused. They were polished, nickel plated or japanned, and finished.

CURRENT CONDITION

Cooper Industries purchased the company in 1976 and moved production to Georgia. Their products are now a part of the Apex Tool Group's catalog.

In 1988, Victory Temple National Holiness Church purchased the property. It functioned as a church and school until 2012. It was then purchased by the Newark-based energy company PSEG in 2013 to be demolished to make way for a switching station. The 177,000-square-foot station functions as an emergency backup to the existing Newark switching station—an inland precaution that became necessary after Hurricane Sandy flooded electrical stations and left Newark households dark. As part of the construction, PSEG conducted an environmental cleanup of the soil to remediate contamination.

Paintings by local artist Kevin Darmanie displayed at the PSEG switching station, 2021

A sculpture by Antonio Perez Melero displayed at the PSEG switching station, 2021

World's Largest Shears Factory Is Marking Century of Service
Jacob Wiss Started Shop in 1848
Everybody's Sewing...at this Easter give
WISS
SCISSORS and SHEARS in SETS
Wiss shears really last
WISS

Rendering of the
Wiss & Sons Exhibit

WISS & SONS EXHIBIT
MEAGAN DAVIS

Collage of *Wiss & Sons Exhibit* graphics

The local community disapproved when the switching station was first announced. They demanded the structure be both beautiful and an asset to the community. Adjaye Associates, the design firm in charge, worked with local firms to propose a 1,790-foot-long enclosure integrated with permanent artwork by fourteen artists supervised by architect Chris Sanders to serve as an "inside-out gallery". The walls were constructed of precast concrete panels that stand thirty-feet-tall with curved perforated aluminum screens painted gold along the top. The walls, a soft red color with horizontal ridges, shorten as they enclose the station revealing more gold with a spiraling effect. The front of the building is lined with thirty-four-foot-tall concrete columns supporting geometric canopies. These cast intriguing shadows, and for this student proposal provide the opportunity to display more artwork, and designate a public space that can function as a community venue.

The *Wiss & Sons Exhibit*, by Meagan Davis, utilizes this design for community involvement and local pride by displaying historical images of the company over its 128 years of operation. Large-print graphics can be adhered to the designated display panels, on the columns and canopies, and display vitrines, or suspended by cables to contribute to the intriguing shadows of this community venue.

The Newark Sunday Times described Wiss and Sons as having "carried the name of Newark to the far corners of the world" with its fine

HISTORY VENDING MACHINES

MEAGAN DAVIS

Rendering of *History Vending Machines*

quality products. Replicas of these products will be available with *History Vending Machines* installed within the exhibit. These vending machines will have large touch screens that allow visitors to browse historical company catalogs, factory photographs over the years, and biographies of Wiss family members, entrepreneurial industrialists and the local workers who made the companies thrive.

Among these biographies you will find Seth Boyden, an inventor with a reputation across many of Newark's thriving industries. Although he died in 1870, his repu-tation is memorialized in Harriet Tubman Park (formerly Washington Park) with a statue and plaque. The *History Vending Machines* of the *Wiss & Sons Exhibit* will also commemorate him with information on his contributions to the history of Newark. He created the American process for manufacturing patent leather which revolutionized the industry and helped Newark become a leather manufacturing center with distinct products like shoes from the James A. Banister Company; he welded high grade crucible steel to a malleable metal which Wiss & Sons developed their "steel-forged" process from to create strong and reliable shears; he took out a patent for a hat body-making machine which was commonly used to manufacture hats to complete the twentieth-century man's outfit; he invented a cut-off switch for steam engines which was used in Watts, Campbell Company's machines and he built a steam engine strong enough to pull locomotives up steep grade as railways continued to expand.

NEWARK'S METAL PRODUCT INDUSTRY

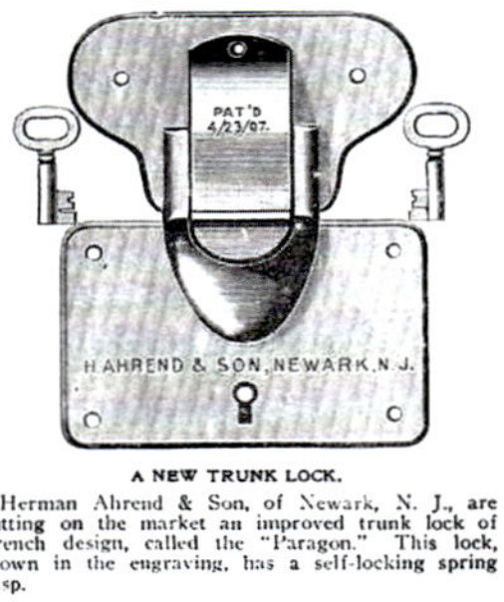

A NEW TRUNK LOCK.

Herman Ahrend & Son, of Newark, N. J., are putting on the market an improved trunk lock of French design, called the "Paragon." This lock, shown in the engraving, has a self-locking spring hasp.

AHREND LOCK FACTORY
179 VAN BUREN ST

BANNISTER A.F. & COMPANY'S CUTLERY MANUFACTORY
FOUNDED 1867
56 SUMMER AVE

C.T. WILLIAMSON WIRE NOVELTY COMPANY
FOUNDED 1876
52-64 BADGER AVE

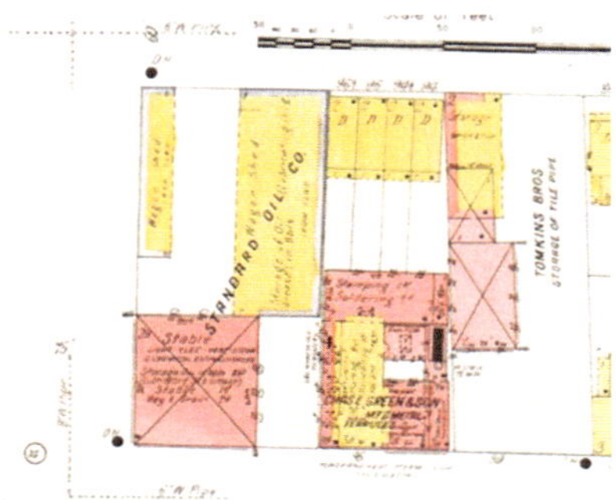

GREEN, CHARLES E & SON
98 CHESTNUT ST, 14 LIBRARY CT,
276 HALSEY ST, 93-97 PASSAIC ST

HAVELL, GEORGE METAL PRODUCTS
284-286 WASHINGTON ST

HEINISCH'S SONS COMPANY
109-123 BRUCE ST

PASSAIC SPRING WORKS
282-292 PASSAIC ST

RALPH HOCHMAN & COMPANY
46-56 EDISON PL

RICHARDSON SAW WORKS
FOUNDED 1890

CRESCENT WATCH CASE COMPANY
FOUNDED 1882, BUILT 1891
65-85 N 13TH ST

D. DELANEY & SON
FOUNDED 1861

GOERTZ, AUGUST & COMPANY
FOUNDED 1904
270-286 MORRIS AVE

HELLER & BROTHERS
FOUNDED 1836
MT. PROSPECT & VERONA AVE

LOWENTRAUT MANUFACTURING COMPANY
FOUNDED 1869
36-54 BRENNER ST

MERGOTT J.E. COMPANY
FOUNDED 1878
316-364 JELLIFF AVE

SCHNEFEL BROTHERS
FOUNDED 1903
684-688 S 17TH ST

VALLEY FORGE CUTLERY COMPANY
FOUNDED 1892
28 S 6TH ST

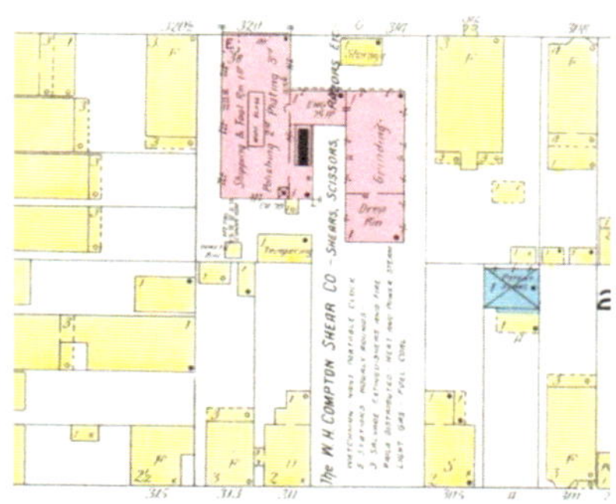

W.H. COMPTON SHEAR COMPANY
314-320 CAMDEN ST
307-309 BERGEN ST

Postcard design by Andrew Engelhardt

POSTCARD DESIGNS

The students included single images as postcards with their projects.

Postcard design by Joseph Ong and Gabriel Castillo

Postcard design by Charles Raimondo

Postcard design by Laurent Gutierrez

Postcard design by James Brett

Postcard design by Elijah Wagner

Postcard design by Ana Torres, Daija Ford, and Hugo Burgos

Postcard design by Meagan Davis

Nina Rappaport is a historian, author, and educator focusing on the integration of industry and urbanism. She is coordinator of the history/theory curriculum at Kean University's School of Public Architecture where she teaches.

She is the author of books on the subject of architecture, urbanism and productive cities including, *Vertical Urban Factory* (Actar 2015 and 2020), co-editor of *Design of Urban Manufacturing* (Routledge 2020), *Hybrid Factory/ Hybrid City* (Actar 2022) and numerous essays. She curated the traveling exhibition *Vertical Urban Factory* in 2011 which has been displayed in 14 venues. Her on-going film project *A Worker's Lunch Box* that features interviews with factory workers received a City Artists Corps grant in 2021.

RESOURCES

Our resources about Newark industry are listed here and include the prime historic publications *Newark, N. J. Illustrated, Newark, the City of Industry*, and *Newark, the Metropolis of New Jersey*, commissioned by the New Jersey Board of Trade.

General Information
Charles F. Cummings New Jersey Information Center, Newark Public Library, https://npl.org/collections-services/charles-f-cummings-new-jersey-information-center/.

Fidelity Union Trust Company, *Historic Newark; A Collection of the Facts & Traditions About the Most Interesting Sites, Streets and Buildings of the City* (Newark: Fidelity Union Trust Company, 1916), https://archive.org/details/historicnewarkco01fide.

Hector, https://hectordesignservice.com/.

Libby, Frank A., *Newark Illustrated 1909-1910* (Newark, 1909).

Mistry, Nisha, Jennifer S. Vey, and Richard Shearer, *Newark's Manufacturing Competitiveness* (Brookings Institute, 2013), https://www.brookings.edu/wp-content/uploads/2016/06/NewarkManufacturingMay28.pdf.

The New Jersey Historical Society, https://jerseyhistory.org/.

New Jersey Institute of Technology, Digital Archive of Newark Architecture, https://dana.njit.edu/.

New Jersey State Chamber of Commerce, *New Jersey; Life, Industries and Resources of a Great State* (Newark, New Jersey State Chamber of Commerce, 1928), Internet Archive, https://archive.org/details/newjerseylifeind00parsrich/page/n3/mode/1up.

Newark, N.J. Board of Trade, *Newark, N. J. Illustrated* (Newark, Wm. A. Baker, 1891), https://library.si.edu/digital-library/book/newarknjillustra00leary.

Newark, N.J. Board of Trade, *Newark, the City of Industry; Facts and Figures Concerning the Metropolis of New Jersey* (Newark, Baker Printing Company, 1912), Internet Archive, https://archive.org/details/newarkcityofindu01newa.

Newark, N.J. Board of Trade, *Newark, the Metropolis of New Jersey* (Progress Publishing Company, 1901).

"Newark Sanborn Maps in the Littman Library," New Jersey Institute of Technology, https://archlib.njit.edu/newark-sanborn-maps-littman-library.

"Sanborn Fire Insurance Map from Harrison and East Newark and Kearny, Hudson County, New Jersey," Library of Congress, https://www.loc.gov/resource/g3814hm.g3814hm_g055011907/?st=gallery.

"Sanborn Maps of New Jersey: Newark," Princeton University, https://library.princeton.edu/libraries/firestone/rbsc/aids/sanborn/essex/newark.html.

Sullivan, S.P., "The most toxic sites in each New Jersey county," NJ.com, updated May 15, 2019, https://www.nj.com/news/2017/04/the_most_toxic_sites_in_each_new_jersey_county.html.

Popper, Samuel H., "Newark, N.J., 1870-1910: Chapters in the Evolution of an American Metropolis." PhD diss., New York University, 1952.

Vail, Merit H. Cash, and Peter J Leary, *Essex county, N.J., Illustrated* (Newark, Press of L. J. Hardham, 1897), *Internet Archive*, https://archive.org/details/essexcountynjill02vail.
Williams, John Austin, *Newark and its Leading Business Men, Embracing Also, Those of Harrison, Kearny, Belleville and Roseville* (Newark, Mercantile publishing company, 1891), *Internet Archive*, https://archive.org/details/newarkitsleading00will.

Zhang, Myles, https://www.myleszhang.org.

Balbach Smelting & Refining Company
"Beer, shears and steam engines," *the Star-Ledger* (May 1998), Newark Public Library, https://knowingnewark.npl.org/beer-shears-and-steam-engines/.

Bennett, J., "Riverbank Park," updated September, 2012, http://www.newarkhistory.com/riverbank.html.

P. Ballantine & Sons Brewing Company
The Architectural Forum, March 1937, p. 179-181.

"Beer, shears and steam engines," *the Star-Ledger* (May 1998), Newark Public Library, https://knowingnewark.npl.org/beer-shears-and-steam-engines/.

Burd, Joshua, "Moving company takes 12,000 sq. ft. at sprawling Newark industrial complex," Real Estate NJ, November 26, 2019, https://re-nj.com/moving-company-takes-12000-sq-ft-at-sprawling-newark-industrial-complex/.

Burd, Joshua, "NAI Hanson named leasing agent at new-look, 807,000 sq. ft. industrial complex in Newark," Real Estate NJ, June 4, 2019, https://re-nj.com/nai-hanson-named-leasing-agent-at-new-look-807000-sq-ft-industrial-complex-in-newark/.

Burd, Joshua, "NAI Hanson: Three new tenants coming to Newark industrial complex," Real Estate NJ, January 10, 2020, https://re-nj.com/nai-hanson-three-new-tenants-coming-to-newark-industrial-complex/.

Burd, Joshua, "Two more tenants commit to Newark industrial campus, taking 59,000 sq. ft.," Real Estate NJ, October 7, 2020, https://re-nj.com/two-more-tenants-commit-to-newark-industrial-campus-taking-59000-sq-ft/.

"From Soup to Nuts to Beer and Snacks, the City Made it All," *the Star-Ledger* (November 1998), Newark Public Library, https://knowingnewark.npl.org/from-soup-to-nuts-to-beer-and-snacks-the-city-made-it-all/.

"In a Glass Darkly: Beer Marks City's History Brewers Benefited from Workers, Water," *the Star-Ledger* (January 1997), https://knowingnewark.npl.org/in-a-glass-darkly-beer-marks-citys-history-brewers-benefited-from-workers-water/.

Knell, Charles E., "Bottling Plant, P. Ballantine and Sons," *The Architectural Forum*, 66, 3, (March 1937): 179-181, *USModernist*, https://usmodernist.org/index-af.htm.

Kofsky, Jared, "280-Unit Development Could Replace Building Around Newark's Old Ballantine Brewery Site," *Jersey Digs*, June 2, 2021, https://jerseydigs.com/280-unit-development-could-replace-building-around-newarks-old-ballantine-brewery-site/.

Borden Dairy Company
"Borden's Farm Products Plant, Newark, N.J.," *The American Architect*, (July 20th, 1928): 125-128. https://dana.njit.edu/files/original/78c3b0edc98bad9c7cf6223f9dd08672.pdf

"From Soup to Nuts to Beer and Snacks, the City Made it All," *the Star-Ledger* (November 1998), Newark Public Library, https://knowingnewark.npl.org/from-soup-to-nuts-to-beer-and-snacks-the-city-made-it-all/.

"The Story Behind the Name: Borden, an American Heritage Brand," Borden Dairy, https://www.bordendairy.com/press-room/history/.

Clark Thread Company
"The Great Chimney at The Clark Thread Works, Kearney [sic], N. J., Height 335 Feet," *Scientific American*, (October 20, 1888): 125.

"The masters of manufacturing: Hyatt, Durand and the Clarks," *the Star-Ledger* (May 1998), Newark Public Library, https://knowingnewark.npl.org/the-masters-of-manufacturing-hyatt-durand-and-the-clarks/.

"Newark Textile Family Wove Threads Through the City's History," *the Star-Ledger* (March 1997), Newark Public Library, https://knowingnewark.npl.org/newark-textile-family-wove-threads-through-the-citys-history/.

Crucible Steel Company of America
Crucible Steel Company of America (Philadelphia: J.B. Lippincott Company, 1925), https://books.google.com/books?id=TblCAQAAIAAJ&printsec=frontcover&source=gbs_ge_summary_r&cad=0#v=onepage&q&f=false.

Hanovia Chemical & Manufacturing Company
"Newark Block bought by Hanovia Company; Manufacturing Firm Assembles Mulberry Street Parcel-- Houses Exchanged," *the New York Times*, March 28th, 1929, https://www.nytimes.com/1929/03/28/archives/newark-block-bought-by-hanovia-company-manufacturing-firm-assembles.html.

Sullivan, S.P., "The most toxic sites in each New Jersey county," NJ.com, updated May 15, 2019, https://www.nj.com/news/2017/04/the_most_toxic_sites_in_each_new_jersey_county.html.

James A. Banister Company
"Five Dead in Gas Pit in Newark Tannery," *the New York Times*, May 22nd, 1933, https://www.nytimes.com/1933/05/22/archives/five-die-in-gas-pit-in-newark-tannery-one-gives-life-in-attempt-to.html.

"Welcome to the original Banister Shoes," Banister Shoes, https://www.banistershoes.org/welcome/index.html.

Murphy Varnish Company
The American Architect, 101, 1904, (June 1912): https://onlinebooks.library.upenn.edu/webbin/serial?id=amarch.

The American Architect and Building News, (September 7, 1889): 6. *Internet Archive*, https://archive.org/details/americanarchitec26newyuoft/page/n877/mode/2up?q=NEWARK.

The American Architect and Building News, (May 4, 1889): 4-5. *Internet Archive*, https://archive.org/details/americanarchitec25newyuoft/page/n681/mode/2up?q=NEWARK.

"Weston and Murphy add sheen to an entrepreneurial tradition," *the Star-Ledger* (May 1998), https://knowingnewark.npl.org/weston-and-murphy-add-sheen-to-an-entrepreneurial-tradition/.

Shifman Mattress Company
James, Gary, "Tradition Reigns at Shifman Mattress," *BedTimes Magazine*, February 15th, 2019, https://bedtimesmagazine.com/2019/02/tradition-reigns-at-shifman-mattress/.

Shifman Mattress Company, https://shifmanmattresses.com/.

Tiffany & Co.
"City's Industrial Past Shines with Jewelry of Gold and Gems," *the Star-Ledger* (May 1997), Newark Public Library, https://knowingnewark.npl.org/citys-industrial-past-shines-with-jewelry-of-gold-and-gems/.

Gray, Christopher, "Prince Street Works," E.R. Butler & Company, https://www.erbutler.com/history/butler/prince_street_works.

"The masters of manufacturing: Hyatt, Durand and the Clarks," *the Star-Ledger* (May 1998), Newark Public Library, https://knowingnewark.npl.org/the-masters-of-manufacturing-hyatt-durand-and-the-clarks/.

Watts, Campbell Company
"Beer, shears and steam engines," *the Star-Ledger* (May 1998), Newark Public Library, https://knowingnewark.npl.org/beer-shears-and-steam-engines/.

Watts, Campbell Company, http://wattscampbell.com/.

Westinghouse Electrical Company
"The 3 W's of Industry: Westinghouse, Waterman and Warehouse," *the Star-Ledger* (June 1998), Newark Public Library, https://knowingnewark.npl.org/the-3-ws-of-industry-westinghouse-waterman-and-warehouse/.

"Westinghouse Concern Plans Extensive Addition," *Newark Sunday Call*, August 14th, 1910, https://news.google.com/newspapers?nid=KjnAay3C9J8C&dat=19100814&printsec=frontpage&hl=en.

"Weston and Murphy add sheen to an entrepreneurial tradition," *the Star-Ledger* (May 1998), Newark Public Library, https://knowingnewark.npl.org/weston-and-murphy-add-sheen-to-an-entrepreneurial-tradition/.

Wiss and Sons Company
"Beer, shears and steam engines," *the Star-Ledger* (May 1998), Newark Public Library, https://knowingnewark.npl.org/beer-shears-and-steam-engines/.

"Scans of Vintage Catalogs, Books, Ephemera, Mementos, Ads, etc.," J. Wiss & Sons Company, http://jwissandsons.com/.

J. Wiss & Sons Co. *Shears, Scissors, Razors, Tinner Snips, Pruning Shears, Cutlery*, 1912.

IMAGE CREDITS

The sources of visual material other than the owners indicated in captions are as follows. Every effort has been made to supply complete and correct credits; if there are any errors or omissions, please contact Vertical Urban Factory so that corrections can be made in any subsequent edition.

All present-day photographs and drawings belong to the authors and students. All Sanborn Maps were accessed through Princeton University, New Jersey Institute of Technology, and the Library of Congress. Printed advertisements were collected from various publications including city directories and *Newark Sunday Call.*

The American Architect: 90
Charles F. Cummings NJ Information Center, Newark Public Library: i, 1, 7, 10, 12, 16, 24, 25, 26, 30-31, 39, 42, 44, 55, 56, 67, 74-75, 78-79, 80, 91, 98, 104, 114-115, 116, 123, 124-125, 126, 127, 129
Consolidated Illustration Company: 72
Essex County Department of Parks, Recreation and Cultural Affairs: 11
Fidelity Union Trust Company: 25
J. Wiss & Sons: 128, 137
J.B. Lippincott Company: 58, 59
Knell, Charles E.: 17, 18
Libby, Frank A.: 77
Newark, N.J. Board Of Trade: 25, 54, 68, 72, 73, 91, 102, 103, 112, 113, 137 (Wm. A. Baker, 1891), 25, 38, 39, 54, 55, 60, 73, 76, 77, 91, 102, 103, 112, 113, 136, 137 (Baker Printing Company, 1912)
Prints and Photographs Division, Library of Congress: 38, 55, 82, 136, 152
Progress Publishing Company: 54, 72, 77, 91, 102, 103, 136
Rappaport, Nina: 22, 43, 47, 130, 131
Shifman Mattress Company: 93, 94, 95
Vail, Merit H. Cash, and Peter J Leary: 24, 137

Newark made a lot—but it distributed a lot too. Volkswagon Beetles arrive at Port Newark, 1965